Published in the United States of America

Visit our Website at www.TheLaptopDancerDiaries.com

ISBN: 1450580203
EAN-13: 9781450580205

Manufactured in the United States of America

Second edition published March 19, 2010
Cover Art ©2010 by Meg Tidd

The Laptop Dancer Diaries is a "mostly" true story. If you think you see yourself in the story and you like it, it's true. If you don't like it, it's the fictional part.

The Laptop Dancer Diaries

A Mostly True Story about Finding Love Again

By Yvette Francino
And Laptop Guy

Dedicated to my parents
Terry and Suzanne Francino

It's because of them
That I've experienced a lifetime of love

Acknowledgements

One piece of feedback I've gotten from some people is that this story should not be "mostly true." It should either be fact or fiction, they say. I'd originally intended for the story to be 100% true – a chance for me to be truly authentic. However, the more I wrote, the more I started getting these funny little qualms about privacy – not just mine, but the privacy of my friends and family.

I wanted this to be a light-hearted story. Let's face it, in order to make something funny, you have to emphasize the embarrassing and often not-so-flattering side of the characters. I changed most of the names and, in some cases, altered a few of the circumstances, but the characters in this book will undoubtedly recognize themselves. For this reason, I would like to issue a big 'Thank you' to all the people who are characters in this book.

For those friends and dates that did not make it into the book, the most likely reason is that you did not provide any embarrassing stories. Please know that it is not a reflection of how much you mean to me.

Thank you to the members of The Boulder Writers Meetup Group who gave me the encouragement to move forward with this project.

Thank you to the many friends and family who have read and critiqued this book. Most notably, I'd like to thank Rebecca Mullen, Jeannine Lee, and Victor Babbitt who gave me chapter-by-chapter advice and insights. You are wonderful friends.

Thank you to my parents. It was your unconditional love that started my life and kept it filled with blessings. I'm so grateful.

Thank you to my family members for bearing with me as I gave more attention to Laptop Guy than to you. Special thanks goes to my daughter, Meg Tidd, who is not only responsible for the cover art, but for motivating me to take this goal of "writing a book" seriously.

I remember an incident from elementary school. It was the first day of third grade and I was lost in the hallways, trying to find my classroom. (Those that know me realize that navigational skills are not my forte, and this was true even at an early age.) My first grade teacher, Mrs. Lehman, saw me and helped me out. Then she gave me this beautiful smile that was so comforting. I thought to myself, "I'm going to remember that smile forever."

Those smiles, whether they come in the form of an encouraging word, a wink, a kind email, a hug – they mean so much. They wrap us in warmth and security. And even the obstacles, hardships and losses, help us grow. Without them, we wouldn't have the joy of overcoming them.

And so, I would like to thank every person in my life. Whether you were in my life only for a moment or for a lifetime, you have made me who I am and have taught me what it means to love. I have finally found my way.

Contents

Prologue

I'm what one might consider a "goal freak." You know the type. We have big life goals broken down to our ten-year-goals. Those are broken down to our yearly goals, monthly, and so on, organized nicely in our organizational tool of choice. We have our missions and visions and we read books like *The 7 Habits of Highly Effective People*.

Yes, that's me. Clearly insufferable, but productive. I can do anything as long as I have a plan. And then day by day, step by step, I execute faithfully, feeling a grand sense of pleasure as I cross off each line item, bringing me closer to my desired end state. Sometimes I'll even write a completed task on my plan, to note the accomplishment and then revel in that happy little feeling from quickly crossing it off as completed.

This system worked wonderfully for the first 43 years of my life. I was accomplishing all of my life goals ahead of schedule. Get Married. Check. Have three incredible kids. Check. Get the perfect job. Check. I was even getting to the "some day before I die" kind of big goals. Run a marathon. Check. Get a Masters Degree. Check. Write a book. Well...before I'm 50, for sure.

Then, in 2003, my husband, a more spontaneous person, told me he wanted a divorce. "Are you crazy?" I asked him. "I have done absolutely no planning for that! It is nowhere on my life's To Do List. It will mess up the entire life plan, not to mention our 20th wedding anniversary party!" I started reading "How to Save Your Marriage" books. I was all set to follow the steps in these books, but, unfortunately, my husband was not interested in doing the requisite partner exercises. I should have realized he wouldn't be up for this. He didn't even want to participate in the "101 Nights of Grrreat Romance" book I'd gotten the year before and that one had much more interesting exercises. So I ended up getting a divorce without doing any planning or preparation.

Being divorced presented a major challenge. I felt it essential to have a husband in order to achieve the "live happily ever after" life plan. Read any fairy tale or romance novel and you will find a loving couple that lives happily ever after. The first task to get back on track

1

would be to fall in love. High achiever that I am, I quickly found a target, and became completely infatuated with someone from work, who I refer to as "FB" in this book. (Yes, the acronym will be explained later.) We started dating and I was ecstatic. I tried again to follow a plan. I read all the books about being sexy and funny and smart and a good girlfriend. I didn't pressure him or nag him or complain about his lack of attention. I gave him his space and waited. But after two years of following what I thought were the right steps, he still didn't fall in love with me. I finally found the courage to break up with him. My 45-year-old clock was ticking.

Three more years passed. I tried online dating, speed dating, and singles groups. I didn't fall in love. Some books say you fall in love when you aren't looking, so I gave that a try. It didn't work. Other experts will tell you to do things you love and you will find love. Nope! Still didn't work. In between these various plans, I sometimes found myself reuniting with FB, in a confusing, uncommitted sort of way, thinking maybe we would end up happily married some day. I haven't read any non-fiction books that recommend that approach for falling in love, but it worked for Big and Carrie in *Sex and the City*.

On New Year's Eve, 2007, I realized the closest thing I had to a boyfriend was my laptop, who I affectionately call Laptop Guy. I was only two years and two months away from turning 50, the day I was sure I'd turn into a wrinkly, shriveled, little old lady with no hope of ever finding love. Clearly there was no authoritative book on the steps required to fall in requited love. I was just going to have to write one myself.

But how would I figure out that magic formula? I'd have to do more than sit around playing with Laptop Guy all day. I'd perform a year-long experiment. I'd have an adventure and at least one date each month. I'd do research by reading books, listening to friends, and taking more risks, recording my observations faithfully in my journals. By the end of the year I would absolutely, positively, without a doubt... be in love.

Yvette just gave me the re-boot. She doesn't think we should see each other so often – our relationship is just too weird. Hey, I get it. I'm a Laptop, she's a person. But in this new world, is that really important? I'm sleek and sexy. Not like that fatso, Desktop Guy. He just sits there in the den, his cables in a big mess under the desk. But me? I travel light. I go with her everywhere. She even brings me into her bed, first thing in the morning or late at night. We really *connect*. She is the only one that turns me on. All it takes is the touch of her finger, and I'm ready to go. She can't just shut me down this way!

January

2008 Resolutions
    1. Have An Adventure Each Month
    2. Fall in Love
    3. Write a Book

January 1

January Goals
    1. Adventure: Rock 'n' Roll Half Marathon in Phoenix
    2. Love: Join Match.Com and Have a January Date
    3. Write: Blog about January Date

It's going to be a great year! I just read *If I'm So Wonderful Why Am I Still Single* and it's got some outstanding insights. I *know* next year at this time I'll be lounging in bed enjoying a lazy New Year's morning with someone I love. (The book says you have to be definite. None of this ambivalent attitude anymore.) My friend, Michael, says you can't *choose* to love someone. He thinks it's unrealistic to have a goal to "Fall in Love." We have discussions about love and relationships every Friday morning. The Starbucks' staff undoubtedly thinks we're a couple as we sit and discuss our latest ups and downs in the singles world each week. We look like a couple. We actually did find each other on *Match.com* about three years ago and dated for a few months. Of all the people I've met on *Match*, Michael and I probably have the most in common. He's 47 years old (just like me), he's a good father (I'm a good mother), his youngest child is Morgan, age 13 (mine is Scotty, age 13), he likes to write (obviously, so do I) and, in my objective opinion, we are both equally smart and good-looking (I'd rate us pretty high on those scales, by the way, in a modest sort of way, of course.) So, why are *we* not in love? Well, probably because when we met each other we had one other thing in common: we were each in love with someone else.

"This time it's going to be different, Michael. I'm definitely going to fall in love this year. If I don't feel that spark immediately, I'm going to give it a chance. It's all in your mind and attitude. You can look for all the loving qualities in a person and *decide* to love them."

"I call that *settling*," argues Michael. "You can't just *decide* to love someone. It's not something you can force."

This is a hot button for Michael. He thinks his soul-mate, Becky, the one he let get away, chose to marry someone else for financial security. Michael has had a very hard time getting over Becky. In fact, even though he hates me to point it out, I think he still idolizes her and will never find anyone else as long as he compares every woman he meets with the perfectly perfect Becky.

Not that I've been much better. I've had my own past love up on a pedestal for far too long. My relationship with FB is over. Since it's over, I probably don't need to clarify that FB stands for Fart Boy, Former Boyfriend, or, more recently – as in the past couple of years – Friend with Benefits. Some people think it stands for F#$k Buddy but that's ridiculous. People that know me realize I can't even drop a proper F-bomb without it sounding completely out of character, so I certainly wouldn't call my only post-divorce relationship a F#$k Buddy. (I can't even write the f#$kin' word!) It doesn't matter anyway because I'm not going to talk about him anymore, ever again, not even in my journal. I'd like to note, however, that FB can also stand for FaceBook, and since I'm such a geek, it is possible that I might use the acronym in that context.

Back to my goals. Despite Michael's skepticism, I think having a goal to fall in love is absolutely appropriate. My plan is to have an adventure and go on at least one *real* date every month. I don't really know exactly *how* I will fall in love – that's why I'm taking all these notes – I'm going to be a real life case study in determining the secret formula. I figure going on an adventure and having a real date each month is a good start. I will resist my natural instincts to find petty flaws with the men I date, and will instead appreciate their attractive qualities. And, of course, because I'm not judging them, they won't judge me and will be blind to all my weird personality quirks. Law of Attraction and all that. Yes, by the end of the year, I am completely confident, I will be in love.

January 2

I'm officially on *Match.Com* again. I've tried online dating sites in the past, but I usually don't last a month. Again, this time it's gonna be different.

It's tempting to lie about my age. I hear every woman over 40 does it. And since seasoned online daters have the reputation of lying, I feel at a disadvantage for being honest. But the *If I'm So Wonderful* book says you have to live the same values that you seek, so I guess I'll 'fess up to my real age.

Birthday: 2/26/60 Age 47
Looking for: Men: 44-50
Tag line: Laptop Dancer

About Me and Who I'm looking For:
My Laptop --I call him "Laptop Guy"-- is my constant companion and I always know how to turn him on! I love computers, enjoy writing, and I spend way too much time online. I do manage to tear myself away from Laptop Guy long enough to enjoy the gorgeous scenery of Boulder. I'm a hiker and a runner. Though I can't say I 'love' running, I do it often enough to be able to reward myself with delicious food and drink, free of guilt.

I have 3 kids--ages 23, 20, and 13, of whom I'm excessively proud. My older kids are out of the house, but my 13-year-old son is with me most of the time and he is one very cool kid. Whenever I have a bad day, he always can make me smile.

I've often thought that I have the luckiest life anyone could ever hope to have--family and friends that I love, great health, an excellent job, and, of course, Laptop Guy. My only complaint is that Laptop Guy is getting old and his performance is, well, lacking. I'm still a vibrant woman and I need more than key strokes. As exciting as it once was to play with Caps Lock and Num Lock keys, I'm past that now.

I signed up for the 6-month Match Guarantee so my profile is always visible, but I don't do the multi-dating thing. To be honest, I rarely have time to date at all.

I'm looking for guys confident and playful enough to join me in an Internet version of "The Dating Game." Once a month, if I'm still looking, I'll play a little game, hope to meet someone new, and blog about it.

January 5

I've been getting a lot of attention from *Match* already! Too bad it's mostly from men that bear a striking resemblance to Mr. Magoo and have screen names like "GardeningGrandpa." I know I'm no spring chicken myself, but it's a sad reality that when an older, unattractive man acts young and silly and flirty, I think, "Ewww. Please go away." When a young, attractive man acts that way, I think, "Ahhh. If only I were younger." When he's an attractive guy my age, I think, "Could this be him?"

Allen is exactly my age (well ... he's 47. I'm trying not to be so picky as to require the same birthday.) His profile sounds excellent... a doctor, two grown kids, no misspellings. (Not that I'm perfect in this regard, but somethin abowt bad spellling jist truns me off!) Allen and I have emailed each other and he has a sense of humor as well. Yes, I've met my Mr. January already! I am doing exceedingly well with my goals! I may be in love before month end! We are going to lunch tomorrow.

January 6

Allen shows up to our meeting place, Jason's Deli, wearing form-fitting workout clothing – the trendy type they sell at the expensive outdoor sports stores like REI. He's thin and, though he's from Denver, he looks like the type of man I see running around the Boulder trails. I try not to be turned off by this. My ex-husband is an extreme sports kind of guy – obsessive about working out – so I tend to go into my "Oh no, he's just like my ex!" panic mode when I see someone wearing expensive workout gear. Allen doesn't know this and I wonder if he's trying to impress me with his running look. One of the things that least impresses me is when someone tries to impress me.

He has little gray, curly chest hairs coming out from under his shirt. He's not unattractive, but I immediately peg him as an arrogant, skinny athlete. He looks a little older than I'd imagined. I have to keep reminding myself that 47 is not so young and he is probably thinking the same thing about me.

I smile at Allen.

7

"You look just like your picture!" he says as we shake hands and stand in line at Jason's Deli.

"So do you!"

We both get the buffet salads. He's eating very healthy stuff. Just like my ex. *I must stop comparing him to Paul, my ex-husband. Healthy is good. Would I rather be dating a fat slob?*

I'd already told Allen in email that my biggest insecurity is my age and that I always feel a bond with fellow 47-year-olds. I'm anxious to let Allen know that I'm not one of those petty women that can't admit to her true age. I may be insecure, but I'm honest!

I figure I might as well address this worry of mine right off the bat. "I've heard women have a reputation for fudging the facts on their profiles, but I haven't found that to be true in men. I haven't met anyone from *Match* that's lied. Have you?"

He looks a little uncomfortable and I feel like I've asked the wrong thing.

He says he's met a lot of women from *Match*.

"How many?"

"About 50."

"Wow!"

He's quick to tell me that of those, there have only been ten or so that went past the first date. The women often look different than their photos. "If they mark on their profile that they're 'average' it's a red flag," he explains, "because the average woman is fat and out of shape. Not true with you at all," he assures me. Obviously, low body fat is important to this guy.

"Do they lie about their age, too?" I ask, out of curiosity, knowing that a lot of women do, but just wondering if the men find out.

"Oh yeah. Of course." he says, in a matter-of-fact way.

"But how do you know?" I ask. "Do you just come out and ask them or do you just assume that they're really older than the age they put in their profile?"

Now he is really hesitating. Maybe he's wondering if I lied and I'm afraid of getting caught. Or maybe he thinks that I think he's being shallow. I want to assure him, *It's OK. I'm really shallow, too!* Or maybe he's just figured out that I really am overly-sensitive about this age thing.

Finally he says, "If I tell you something, you won't write it in your blog, will you?"

"Oh no!" I assure him. "I'd let you read anything in my blog before I published it." *No need to mention my tell-all book plan.*

"OK. The truth is I'm really 53. But from a biological perspective, I've got the health of someone that's younger than 47."

Well, whoop-de-do! That's six whole years! Biologically, I have the health of someone younger than 41, but I didn't put that age in my profile! Hey... I'm in better shape than I was at 15! (Admittedly, that's because I was a lazy couch-potato kid. But still!) I'm shocked that he didn't tell me his true age when we'd bonded over our shared 1960 birthdays. I don't care about his low-body-fat-aerobically-fit-physique. I want someone who's 47! Or at least someone who's honest about his age. I realize I'm being a bit overdramatic about this, but, I can't help it. I haven't yet learned the fine art of choosing to love someone.

January 8

My friend, Chet, meets me at 8:00am for our final long workout before the half-marathon. We've braved the Colorado cold every Saturday for the last three months, but this morning we're hitting the treadmills at the Broomfield Rec Center. Chet takes off his sweatpants exposing his massive calves. I tease him that his calves are so huge they should be called cows.

Chet's new to running. We met on a hike last summer, right after he and his wife separated. We talked and I recommended a divorce recovery seminar series based on Bruce Fisher's book, R*ebuilding When Your Relationship Ends.* I actively volunteer and socialize with members of the *Rebuilder* community (people that have been through the seminars) and Chet and I have become friends. I was pleasantly surprised when Chet took me up on the suggestion to start running and even more surprised when he decided to go with me to Phoenix to run the P.F. Changs Rock'N'Roll half-marathon! It may be a Nike slogan, but Chet lives by the motto: "Just Do It!" I love that about him!

Chet does not have a runner's body – another plus in my book. He's stocky and muscular. Looks much more like a wrestler than a runner. He's got a sailor tattoo on his right bicep and Taz tattooed on one of those oversized calves. He's gregarious and cute, a former bad boy and huge flirt. Chet is eight years my junior and though he's a great flirtatious friend, we really are just buddies. I've encouraged him to get on *Match*, too. He hasn't gotten nearly the attention that I thought he would – I guess because he's a guy and not officially divorced. He's ready to play, though. There's no chance of reconciliation with his wife and he's just waiting for the paperwork to become officially single.

We compare notes on our recent dates.

I'd set him up with a friend of mine. He liked her, but they didn't click. Chet likes Harley chicks. Teresa was more of an academic type – kind of like I used to be in my younger days. Like when I was 46.

Now it's my turn to tell Chet about my lunch date with Allen.

"He was a nice guy, but no sparks."

"Are you going out again?"

"Maybe after we get back from Phoenix..." I say in my usual unenthusiastic tone. Chet knows there is an unspoken "but I don't want to" at the end of that sentence.

"I always do this. I'm overly picky and never give anything a chance. This year I'm going to have at least one "real" date a month and blog about it. I've already committed to my blog readers and I can't give up in the first week of January."

"How many blog readers do you have?"

"That's not the point." (Unfortunately, Allen is most likely my only blog reader and I'm sure he's anxiously awaiting a review.) "I made a commitment to myself and I'm going to do this!"

"I'd be a good date, Baby."

"I bet you would, Boy Toy."

"How about we go to the Kool and the Gang concert after the race and I can be your January date?"

"You sure you're up for that, Babe? I might be too hot for you to handle."

Chet and I call each other names like *Baby*. It's all part of our flirt game.

He says he's sure. He wants to see what I'd say in my blog about him.

10

"Right now I'm out with a hot, young, hunk that took his pants off and we got all sweaty together, so if nothing else, I can blog about this and make it sound pretty steamy."

"You think this is good," he jokes. "Just wait!"

Chet and I are having fun. I emailed him a flirty poem and he returned the favor. Could he be even a tad serious? Might something happen in Phoenix? I am trying to take more risks. According to the *If I'm SO Wonderful* book, men eight years your junior are perfect. Statistically, you die at the same time.

From: Yvette Francino <yvette.francino@gmail.com>
To: Chet Hunkyman <boytoy@yahoo.com>
Sent: Monday, January 8 7:23:26 PMSubject: Poem

For you, Babe....

Calf Lust

It was on a hike that I first met
My favorite Boy Toy. His name is Chet.

His calves were the thing I noticed first
Muscles so big, I thought they'd burst!

More of those legs I had to see
So I invited Chet to run with me.

On the treadmills I got my chance
To gaze with awe when he dropped his pants.

I wondered if it would be too much
If I asked perhaps to have a touch.

Like a man, I was obsessed
Only men prefer to feel breasts.

I settled for a first rate view
Of the bulging muscles and tattoo.

My breathing quickened, my heart beat fast
I didn't think that I could last.

I'd never been on such a date
I blamed the run for my weak state.

I soon knew I needed more
I figured out when I could score.

I had a plan for the Phoenix race
That would surely get me past first base.

Virgin legs will need some care
In order to properly prepare

Massaging will be instrumental
My hands are ready to be gentle.

And when the race at last is done
Those burning legs will have had their fun.

From: Chet Hunkyman <boytoy@yahoo.com>
To: Yvette Francino <yvette.francino@gmail.com>
Sent: Tuesday, January 9 6:41:15 PM
Subject: Poem

Response to Calf Lust

Calf Lust is great you sexy lass
If they're that good imagine my ass.

I'm glad we ran when I lost my pants
It's your turn now to do a dance.

My calves are here for you to touch
But don't stop there that ain't enough.

My calves, although big, have one tattoo
there's a lot more to see and I dare you.

It's funny that you brought up breasts
you're right you know, guys are obsessed.

If you think running takes your breath away
then you're in for quite a surprise one day.

To Phoenix we go, I'd like to explore
if memory serves you're a size four.

See you soon my running mate
Phoenix is sounding like one hot date.
  ~theBoytoy

When it comes to sex, my Inner Devil and Inner Angel are always giving me conflicting advice.

Devil: Have you ever seen bigger muscles? Look at those tattoos! You know you've always wanted to seduce a guy. Here's your chance!

Angel: He's going through a very vulnerable time right now. He's not thinking straight.

Devil: All the better! You'll never have it so easy! You won't even have to be any good and he'll probably think you're a sex queen.

Angel: He's not even divorced yet. You are his friend, not his lover.

Devil: You're all talk, no action. Stop being such an old lady.

Angel: Don't listen to him, Dear. You were a little Goody-Goody even when you were young.

Most of the time the irritating angel wins, reminding me of my Catholic upbringing and virtuous ways. But, damn it! It's 2008, and time to take risks and do things differently. My "sexy-years" are numbered and if I'm ever going to join the ranks of experienced seduction queens, I'd better get moving. If I keep listening to that angel, I'll end up the classic little ol' lady darning socks, with no book to write or stories to tell.

Having just run the half-marathon (at a personal best at 2:02:34, I might add), I'm feeling fit, though my toes are not looking good. (Reminds me of the old joke about tolio. The one where the guy has mangled toes (tolio), gnarley knees (kneasles), and when he removes his pants she says, "Don't tell me. Small cox?") Despite my plans to sexily saunter, I'm looking a little gimpy as I hobble to the bar with Chet for drinks before the concert. I'm not to be discouraged, though. Alcohol is always great for multiplying my perceived sexiness and the sexiness of all those around me.

Things are going quite nicely. There's some football game playing at the bar that I pretend to be interested in. Chet and I are chatting with the locals. Everyone's joking and having a good time.

14

A new character enters the scene. Since I want to protect her privacy, I'll just call her "Bitch." Truly, she is not really a Bitch, but I like calling her that because even when I'm drunk, that's as vile as I get with name-calling. Bitch is actually pretty tame for what I'm thinking.

She's 28 years old, loud, and an attention hog. She and her friend, a quieter woman (which really isn't saying much since everyone in the bar is quieter than Bitch), saunter (yes, they saunter...apparently, their toes are fine) into the bar and she immediately starts yakking away, flirting with most of the men, including, of course, Chet. Chet does not seem bothered by this in the least. In fact, I do believe that he's enjoying it to the point of wanting to push me under the table.

Funny, that I can go from "date" to "third wheel" in a matter of minutes. Chet scoots a little further from me and makes sure the bar room conversation reflects the fact that we're "friends" and not more. Bitch has no trouble getting herself and her friend invited along on my "date of the month" to the concert.

I make a quick call and invite another friend, Craig, to join. Craig's great. He's got this intensely spiritual side – one of the only Catholics I know that can quote the Bible. (Most of us are good at memorizing prayers, but don't really know too many Bible verses.) But Craig is just downright *good*, right to the core. However, at the oddest moments he'll come up with a risqué remark which is especially hilarious because it seems so out of character. I hadn't originally asked him to join us – he has a girlfriend and this was *supposed* to be my big January date, but obviously it appears to be turning into a group event. Craig's in Phoenix on business and had asked me to give him a call when I was here. With him along at least the male/female ratio will be a little better and I'll get some male attention.

As I limp to the concert, feeling about as sexy as a wounded dog, I hear Bitch talking about some "50-year-old dirty old man" that's after her. (I think this is enough to turn off Craig who is close to 50 himself, so I now have an ally in my distaste for Bitch.) She's quite drunk by this time and obviously thoroughly smitten with her own

15

humor and sex appeal. Chet, similarly imbibed, is entertained and enjoying the attention from Bitch and her friend. I'm not entertained in the least. Having sobered up, I realize there will be no seduction moves tonight. At least not from me!

Angel: I'm sorry, Dear, but, you know it was for the best.
Devil: Wuss... You could at least have a nice little cat fight.
Another disappointing night.

January 14
As I sit in a Phoenix café, I amuse myself with a pleasant daydream of Bitch vomiting violently in Chet's face. Chet's supposed to meet me here, but after last night, I'm not sure I even want to have breakfast with him. Here he comes now, with a big smile on his face, energetic and happy as ever.

"Hey, Baby! How'd you sleep?"

Baby? The Baby talk is OFF! Does he actually think I'm going to flirt with him? Does he even realize what a jerk he was last night? I think I'll tell him.

"You were a jerk last night."

Chet looks surprised.

"How could you invite that drunk, obnoxious tramp on what was supposed to be *our* date?"

"Well.... She asked if she could come with us. What was I supposed to say?"

"No."

"But she really liked me."

I forgot Chet is newly single. He's flattered by attention. The more the better. I'm sure he figured there was enough of him to go around for all the ladies.

"That was supposed to be my special date of the month! You were going to be 'Mr. January' in my book! You weren't supposed to invite some loud-mouth attention-stealing skank to join us."

"I gave you my coat," Chet reminds me, as though this chivalrous act should be enough to prove he's a good date. It is true that I was cold and his big leather jacket felt good, but I'm not about to forgive him.

"You weren't treating me like a date. You were treating me like a frail old lady who needs a coat to keep warm."

"That's not how I treated you."

"You acted like you wanted to get rid of me! Like I was this third wheel on a date that you were trying to have with the Bitch!" I'm exaggerating a little here to make a point. It seems to be working because Chet looks very distraught.

"I am so, so, sorry. I would never want to hurt you. Your friendship means everything to me."

OK, maybe I laid the guilt on a little too thick.

"It's OK," I tell him, softening.

"No it's not. I hurt you. I told you I'd be your Mr. January and I messed everything up. I'm a terrible friend."

Now, I'm actually worried that Chet's thinking I have some major crush on him. The truth is, Chet and I both like the flirt game, but I don't think either of us ever really wanted to take it past flirtation, yet neither wanted to be the one to back down. It might have gotten very awkward if Bitch hadn't come along and stolen the show. In some ways, I guess, I'm a little relieved. Chet's like a cute, younger brother to me and it would have been out of line for me to mess that up. Had I actually tried to seduce him, I'm sure it would have ended up very embarrassing and awkward for us both.

"You're not a terrible friend. I know we were just playing. I like to flirt and you're good at flirting back. I'm all talk and no action, anyway. I'm sure you had better luck with the Bitch."

"Well, she lives in Chicago, but she says she's going to call me, and she's already sent me a text," Chet tells me proudly. Though I still feel a tad jealous, I've completely forgiven him. I can see he's very sorry and he really is quite cute. He's like a puppy, excited and happy about his new single status, and I'm genuinely happy for him.

But the whole situation did start me examining my "flirt buddy" behaviors that I enjoy with a few male friends. These are friends with whom I have no physical relationship, but I tease them, ogle them, tell them they're cute, and generally give them the impression that I'm interested in more than friendship. I'm quite skillful at coming up with suggestive innuendos and I more than enjoy reciprocal attention. But the truth is that I rarely, if ever, follow through, even with as much as a kiss.

17

I'm most skilled in the art of flirtation via email – hence, my "Laptop Dancer" nickname. It seems when I am safely on my computer, I can be quite witty. I successfully deliver just the right amount of suggestiveness to leave the recipient confused about my intentions. Am I just playing or could there be an element of truth behind my teases? Even I don't always know. I enjoy the game and Chet is good at playing it, but, as last night taught me, it does have its pitfalls.

Chet and I agree that ground rules to our game are in order.

"When we go out, we have to decide whether we're going out as wing men or flirt buddies. If we're playing wing men, we can flirt with other people. As flirt buddies, we should give priority attention to each other."

"Sounds good," Chet agrees. "So can we be flirt buddies now?" he asks, "Because you're really looking a lot like a sexy, temptress Laptop Dancer."

"It's a deal, you hunky Boy Toy."

Chet smiles as we clink our coffee mugs in a toast.

And so I end my adventure on a breakfast date with full attention from my young, hot friend. I guess Boy Toy, Chet, is a good Mr. January after all.

Yvette has been on me more than ever. All this *Match.com* email. I've been filtering most of it for her. Major compatibility issues with these guys. Maybe she'll start to realize she has it pretty good with ol' Laptop Guy. I even have a spell-checker. Admittedly, our relationship isn't perfect. To be perfectly frank, I've been checking out the gURLs, trying to get a few IP addresses myself, but it's risky business out in the cyberworld. Some nasty viruses getting passed around out there!

February

February Goals

    1. Adventure: Cancun
    2. Love: Fling in Mexico (??)
    3. Write: Gather.com

I'm excited! I'm finally feeling the hint of the butterflies! Yippee! I've decided to go to Cancun for my February Adventure and have invited several friends. A really cute guy from my past is interested in joining me!

February 4

"Are you really going this time?" Michael knows I've bailed on trips for the past two winters. Not that he ever offers to go with me. I crave the sunshine, but a romantic setting with no man? That would just be depressing.

"I've paid the non-refundable deposit and bought my airline tickets. I'm going for sure. And guess what? It looks like I'll be going with a hot Mr. February. Marmer. Remember him?"

"Marmer? I sort of remember the weird name, but I don't remember the story."

"He's that guy that sent me a picture of his butt a couple of years ago."

"Oh yeah. Did he just sit on the copy machine and Xerox it or what?"

"No! It was very tasteful. It was a picture of him looking over his shoulder into the mirror at his naked very muscular gluteus maximus in his private weight room."

"Sounds like an ass to me."

"Yeah... Well... He *may* be a little full of himself, but his emails have been very sweet. He says he's always wanted to go to Mexico and has been waiting ten years until he could go with a beautiful woman. He's not going to let this opportunity pass him by. Isn't that romantic? Although I'm not entirely sure if he's saying I'm beautiful or that he's just tired of waiting to go to Mexico."

"What's with the name? Sounds like a farmer. Marmer the Farmer?"

"Michael! He's VERY hot. A body builder! And he's an engineer, not a farm boy. Marmer is short for Larrimore, which is kind of a... *I choose my word carefully*... sophisticated name. He's smart and funny."

"Are you seriously able to look him in the face and call him 'Marmer' without cracking up?"

"OK, OK. I hate his name! And now when I do say his name, I'll remember this conversation and probably have some goofy look on my face, so let's stop talking about it! He doesn't look like a Marmer at all."

I'm ashamed to discover I'm a name bigot. How many times have I been annoyed with people for having trouble with my name and questioning why I "go by" Yvette? I "go by" Yvette because that's the name my parents picked! It wasn't like I had any say in it. People pronounce it and spell it in all kinds of crazy ways. Because I've been a victim of name bigotry myself, I certainly did not want to impose this ridiculous judgment on Marmer. Still, I'd prefer to call him Mr. February in my book. Marmer doesn't sound sexy and he is a very sexy guy.

"So what are the rooming arrangements going to be on this trip?"

"He's been trying to convince me to room with him, but I hardly know him."

"What about your 2008 goals to be more bold?"

"I said I was going to be bold, not a slut! I'm getting a single room, so if it happens that things develop, I'll be ready. I think it's pretty bold just to go to Mexico at all without a wingman. Are you sure you don't want to go? It's a singles thing, so there should be plenty of hot chicks that dig you." Michael often reminds me that chicks dig him.

"No thanks. I'm sure you'll have your *hands* full with Marmer."

"Yeah," I say tentatively. "Do you think it's weird that he wears a leopard-skin G-string?"

"Seriously?"

"I'm not really sure. When he was trying to convince me to room with him, he said he wanted to tease me by running around in his leopard-skin G-string. I couldn't tell if he was kidding. I told him that I was really more of a boxers-kind-of-gal."

"Did you also tell him you talk to your laptop?"

"I don't REALLY talk to my laptop." *Not out loud, anyway...*

"You have *met* Marmer, haven't you? He's not just one of those *Match.com* guys that you've only emailed and exchanged butt photos with?"

"We didn't *exchange* butt photos. He sent a butt photo to me and I sent him an obviously doctored up photo with my face on the top of a Victoria Secret's model. And *yes*, we have met. We went out a couple of times in the end of 2005. Confident. Good kisser. "

"Did you tell him how you're NOT going to have sex with him?" Michael never passes up an opportunity to remind me what a downer it was (literally) when I'd once used that line on him. During the brief period of time that Michael and I'd dated...right around the same time I'd met Marmer, come to think of it...we'd never had sex. But that was back in the days when I was a Goody Two Shoes and thought you had to be in love to have sex.

"I think there's a very good chance I'll have sex with Mr. February" I proclaim.

February 10

Mr. February seems to have disappeared. The price has gone up for Mexico and Marmer hasn't gotten his tickets. I don't understand what happened. I'm usually really intuitive about these kinds of things and Marmer was not giving me any clues that he was losing interest. In his last email he told me he couldn't wait for "our vacation." In situations like this, I've found the best course of action is to send a multiple choice quiz. I sent Marmer the following email:

From: Yvette Francino <yvette.francino@gmail.com>
To: Marmer Ass masshole@comcast.net
Sent: Monday, February 10 7:23:26 PM
Subject: Where are you?
Hi Marmer,
I've sent you a few emails and I haven't heard back from you. I'm sure you're fine, but just in case, maybe you could let me know if you get this email? To save you time, here are several responses you can choose from to let me know why I haven't heard from you:
A) I had a nightmare about you. Go away.
B) I got hit by a truck.

22

C) You are such a vision of beauty that I could not bear to be in Mexico unless we roomed together.
D) I've fallen head over heels in love with you and I know you'll break my heart so I had to cut off all communication.
E) Laptop Guy has obviously been intercepting all my email to you and is deleting it.
F) I have found a hot woman that will room with me in Mexico. See you there.
G) I am broke and can't afford either Mexico or my Comcast bill so I have no access to email.
H) I only have leopard-skin g-strings and you prefer boxers.
I) When I learned you wouldn't room with me, I went into a state of deep depression.
J) Other_____ (Feel free to make up a really good lie.)

If I don't hear back from you, I will worry that something's wrong, so please email back, even if it's just a short little note to tell me all is fine and that you just got busy with other things.

February 12

Marmer hasn't replied.

However, FB finally has IM'ed me. I know I'm not supposed to talk about him, but I think it's important to note that I did not give in to my previous pattern of running right back into his bed. I figured he eventually would contact me. I know I should have blocked him but... That would mean I care enough about him to avoid him. I don't mind that he contacts me. I just need to be strong. He was drunk. Said he'd drunk a bottle of wine because there was no soda in his house. No mention at all of the three months of no communication. I told him I was going to Mexico next week and he wanted to know if I was going with anyone. It was tempting to brag about Marmer, but I restrained myself. It's best not to brag about a hot guy with a weird name who has totally blown you off. FB asked me about *Match.com*. The fishing for information about love life usually opens up a discussion of availability. I did not take the bait, though, and kept it friendly, but not flirtatious. I'm very proud of myself. It's Valentine's week and I appear to be without a Mr. February. Despite my natural instinct to beg FB to go with me to Mexico, I played it cool. Yup. FB can just drink his wine and drown in his tears 'cause he missed his chance with me. This ship has sailed.

February 13

I check the obituaries. Marmer must be dead. It's the only explanation that makes sense.

February 14

Valentine's Day spent with a young cutie. Scotty gave me this little gold chain bracelet. I was with him when he won it with one of those claw machines at Dave & Busters.

"I thought you were going to give this to Trixy for her birthday!" Trixy is Scotty's step-Mom. The woman my husband left me for. I'm sure she's a very nice lady even though the thought of her ties my stomach in knots. And though I really try to avoid thinking or saying anything negative about her, I admit that I do take guilty pleasure in the fact that the name, Trixy, conjures up images of prostitutes or dogs. But she is Scotty's step-Mom so that's as much as I'll sully her name.

"I wanted to give it to *you* because of what it says."

I examine the bracelet closely. Lightly engraved are the words, "I Love You." Tears come to my eyes. Scotty doesn't know (I hope) how lonely I am when he's at his Dad's. I get in my moods of feeling so alone – like no one needs me or loves me. The sweet bracelet and the reminder that I'm loved is just what I need on this Valentine's Day. I'm the luckiest Mom ever.

February 15

I've decided gather.com, a social media site catering to people who like to write, is better than blogging when working on my writing. It's not quite as public as a blog and I've made some virtual friends that can give me advice about writing. It was thanks to this site that Laptop Guy came to life last year.

I found that I rather liked personifying inanimate objects with my writing on gather.com. I got a kick out of taking any object and coming up with a fitting personality. I especially liked making the objects edgy and sexy, filled with innuendo. I call this inanimitacy. Inanimate intimacy. The shoes that got together, their laces tangled, ended up having quite the make out session...lots of tongue involved.

There were family stories, too, and even some drama with the flaky snow-teen, who, along with her entire family, melted at season's end.

Laptop Guy gave me perfect fodder for clever puns and sexual innuendo. I don't want to get too graphic, but you can really take it quite far when you talk about joy sticks and plugging into USB ports. Since I joked so often about my intimate relationship with Laptop Guy, I thought it might be fun to create an account for him, too. Gather's encouragement of alter-egos and multiple accounts, gave me the perfect opportunity to get in touch with my inner-bad-boy personality. I found a sexy Brad Pit lookalike photo on the internet. It's an arrogant "I think I'm so cool" photo of this muscle-ripped guy lying on a bed with a sleeveless T-shirt, one arm tucked behind his head on the pillow. Making that the wallpaper for my laptop, I was able to create an image of a laptop with a sexy upper half which would become "Laptop Guy's" icon.

When I log into the site as "Laptop Guy", I banter with "Yvette F." (This is the "real" me with my own photo.) Today, for example, I posted an article about not really wanting to go to Mexico alone. Then I logged on as Laptop Guy, who made some lewd comments about his "hard disk." He also tells me if I'd get off my ass instead of playing on the computer all day, maybe I'd actually find a human to go with me to Mexico.

Most of my virtual friends are aware that Laptop Guy and Yvette F are both me, but today my brother, Neal, has logged into Gather. He knows I spend a lot of time on the site and he was perusing it to see what I'd been up to. This, in itself, is cause for alarm. I write quite a bit of personal stuff that I really need time to edit before opening it up to family! It's one thing to write about joy sticks in a suggestive way when you think no one you know will ever read it, but if your brother reads it, he may come and confiscate joysticks or any other phallic-shaped objects he can find in your house.

Neal decides to join into the conversation I'm having with "Laptop Guy."

"Where do you get off telling my sister to get off her ass, you arrogant son of a bitch!"

Neal writes me a private email asking me why I'm even bothering to respond to "Laptop Guy" and that I should block him immediately.

Charmed by his protectiveness, but overwhelmingly amused at Neal's anger, I call him up.

"Laptop Guy is really *me*," I explain.

"What are you talking about?"

"I just made him up. He's kind of a geeky, sexy alter ego."

Neal didn't understand me at first. I'm not sure if this was because I was laughing so hard or because it is hard to understand why someone would create, let alone engage in conversation, with an arrogant laptop.

All he said was, "Yvette.....you need help."

February 20

On the flight to Cancun, I'm reading *Eat, Pray, Love*. This is a really interesting book and it's a huge best seller. And it's even kind of like my book – a true life memoir about a divorced women's search for self-discovery. Of course, Elizabeth Gilbert is much more spiritual than I am. Maybe I'll name my book, *Eat, **Play**, Love*. And that's what I'm going to do on this trip. Eat, play, and fall in love! Or at least find a Mr. February!

February 20 7pm

It's surprising that in this nationally advertised "Singles Travel" vacation, there are only seven of us who have signed up – five women and two men. This is quite a different scenario than the hoards of dirty old men that I've been imagining. Amazingly, the men, Tom and Rick, are even attractive! Everyone is friendly. I take an instant liking to Jessica who's doubling with Debbie in the room next to mine.

We all meet in the resort bar for drinks and dinner.

Tom and Rick are friends who have traveled down from Boston together. They're rooming together and look very fit. They play tennis. Debbie has already suggested to the other women that she thinks the men are gay. They haven't done the typical "latching on to the best looking woman" thing that men do at singles events, but since there are only seven of us, this, thankfully, is not a typical singles event.

I enjoy flirting with cute men, regardless of whether or not they're romantically interested in me. I've discovered that the less available a man is the more heavily I flirt. Maybe because it's obvious it's just a game which makes it more "safe."

I cut quickly through the chit chat and get right into mildly flirtatious behavior. I figure I might as well settle this question of sexual orientation quickly. I don't have much time to find a Mr. February. The thing about the flirt game is you have to test the waters slowly to see if anyone wants to play. I tell the group about *The Laptop Dancer Diaries*. It's a good way to start prying into – I mean, exploring – the personal lives of others.

Me: "I'm writing a book about my 2008 adventures and people I meet along the way. You guys might end up as intriguing characters. What juicy secrets can you tell me?"

Tom: "Do they have to be true?"

Me: "They have to be interesting."

Tom: "I used to be a woman."

This comment would seem to tip the scales toward the gay side, but Tom is saying this in a cute, conspiratorial way, whispering the "secret" and enjoying the attention from me which points more towards straight. I think. In any case, I'm quite sure he's never been a woman. Very good possibility for Mr. February.

I continue to pry for more evidence.

Me: "The book is about relationships. I'm going to have an adventure and a date each month and write about it. Mexico is my February Adventure." I tell them how I use *Match.com* to help find dates and that I make a game out of it to make it more palatable. I give people "compatibility points" to figure out who I'll go out with.

Rick: "I don't like game-players. And please don't write about me in your book."

This comment indicates that regardless of whether or not Rick is gay, he does not want to play with me. I try to explain that it's a very innocent "game." It's not like I'm being dishonest, but Rick thinks any dating games are immature. Thumbs down on Rick as a potential Mr. February.

The conversation continues amongst the group with some sharing of dating stories, primarily from the women. The sexual orientation of the men remains ambiguous. They share a few dating stories and we discover that Rick was once married. I'm guessing "straight" but my gaydar isn't good and they seem to be keeping their cards close to the vest.

February 22

Today we went to the Chichen Itza Mayan ruins. These Ruins have recently been voted one of the new wonders of the world, so I'm glad to have my adventure of the month be more profound than drinking margaritas on the beach. I would not have voted it worthy of one of the seven wonders of the world, myself, but that may have been because some big cleaning-of-the-steps was going on at the Pyramids and we couldn't even climb to the top. I was outraged to learn that the ancient Mayans threw their children into these wells as a sacrificial offering because their tears would appease the rain God. That alone should have disqualified this particular site for the mere absurdity of that ritual. Someone should have clued these guys in to the fact that dead kids can't cry. They would have gotten a whole lot more tears out of the kids just by threatening to take away whatever was the equivalent of a Mayan video gaming system.

In any case, I'm proud to report that I'm making slow but steady progress with my flirt game, though I still have no idea whether or not the men are gay or straight. Jessica, Tom, Rick and I have been hanging out together since we've been in Mexico and it's been fun. Even Rick has a playful side and has warmed up to me, though he's still a little tentative.

"I'm going to name you **Alfred** in my book" I tease him.

"You are NOT going to write about me in your book." He puts on a fake mad face.

"I can write whatever I want. It's my book!"

"If you write about me, my name better not be **Alfred**! I don't look like an **Alfred**!"

"Yup, **Alfred**. That's you!"

February 23 7pm

At dinner, our travel agent, Cheryl, presents the men with a bottle of tequila she'd won earlier today at bingo.

"I'm giving this to Tom and Rick because they're the cutest couple," she announces.

A not-so-subtle way of finally getting the answer the women had been debating since the trip began.

"Cutest COUPLE????" They are both very surprised and insulted. "We are NOT gay!"

This is followed by a lot of embarrassment and nervous laughter from both the men and the women further followed by a relatively heated debate about the injustice of the women assuming the men were gay.

Men: "Just because we don't act like pigs, you assume we're gay?"

Women: "Well, you ARE rooming together."

Men: "Women room together all the time and no one assumes they're gay."

I'm tempted to tease them with one of those "Methinks the straight-guys doth protest too much" lines, but I remember that people usually get annoyed when I pull the "Methinks" quote. Instead I assure them that I never believed for a second they were gay. It's all Debbie's fault for spreading around some rumor that they were celebrating an Anniversary! (Apparently, a totally unsubstantiated piece of gossip.)

The truth is, I'm still not completely convinced they're straight, but one fortunate outcome of all this debate is that the men now seem anxious to convince us they are, indeed, straight. This equates to extra attention for the ladies, particularly Jessica and me.

Jessica is beautiful. Not only is she this wholesome, funny, gorgeous woman, she just has this goodness about her. There are just some people you meet in your life that you immediately like, and Jessica is one of those for me. She's deeply religious and we've had some good discussions about Christianity. I was a little worried about Jessica disapproving of me and my book. I mean it is partly about getting in touch with my inner-devil. But she's not at all judgmental. She likes teasing the guys as much as I do, usually with a little smirk on her face – kind of like a wink, without really being a wink. I consider for a split second whether or not Jessica would make a good Mr. February. Nah. Not ready for that yet. But I swear, if I were a straight guy, I'd be so smitten.

Rick and Tom suggest going out to a disco for salsa dancing with Jessica and me. Though salsa dancing is not particularly a manly man type of activity, I think this is another attempt on Rick's part, to prove his manhood. Rick acts a little like it's a double date, though not clear who would be with whom. Based on our seating, if I were looking at it as an outsider, I'd still guess Rick and Tom were one couple and Jessica and I were the other couple. Not exactly "wild" but I'll take what I can get.

February 23 Midnight

We've spent most of the night looking for a salsa club that Rick's friend told him about. After three bus rides and wandering for several blocks through the streets of Cancun, we find the club. It's all boarded up. No salsa tonight. Fine with me. I don't know how to salsa anyway. We've been laughing and talking the whole evening. Such a fun evening with new friends even though we did nothing but search for a closed-down salsa club.

February 24

_____ After dinner, I wander into the main lobby of the resort, heading for the computer room to feed my email addiction. Before I can get on a computer, though, I'm stopped by a man who has just arrived that day at the resort. He's a young, black guy with a baby face wearing a touristy Hawaiian shirt and some dorky shorts. He makes small talk, anxious to start his partying, and wants to know if I'll come up to his room and show him where the alcohol is kept.

Not being one to experience the bar scene often, I'm not sure if this is a pickup. Many years ago, when computer games were in their infancy, there was a hilarious adventure game starring a dorky guy named "Leisure-Suit Larry," an Austin Powers kind of character. This guy has that same sleazy aura to him, but maybe he just legitimately wants help finding his alcohol. Wait a minute. That's what hotel personnel are for. I deduce it must be a pickup.

Devil: Duh! Of course it's a pickup! Even if he just wants to party, go up to his room and seduce the guy! Here's your Mr. February! How much easier can it get?

Angel: Darling, there are DISEASES out there! Especially in Mexico!

Devil: Don't listen to her. Opportunities like this aren't going to come again. Now get up to that room!

I briefly weigh the options. I'm on vacation, single, and will never have to see this guy again. The Devil is making some good points – and I do really want to accomplish my goals. Maybe if he took off the dorky clothes, he would be more appealing. I imagine it for a second. Nope -- I have absolutely no attraction for this guy. Going to his room would be the stupid act of an insecure ninny. The Angel wins again.

"No thanks" I tell the boy-man. "I don't go to the rooms of men I don't know." I say it with a smile. I don't want to be rude and it is mildly flattering that this young guy picked me amongst the crowd, even if he is a doofus.

"So, let's get to know each other. Join me for a drink."

It's a minor concession. I don't want the Devil to be totally ashamed of me. I can at least have a drink with the guy. We walk over to the resort bar. Drinks are complimentary so I don't have to think about whether he'll expect any kind of repayment for this invitation.

As we drink, "Leisure-Suit Larry" makes some not-so-subtle suggestions about how we can "have more fun."

"I'm flattered, but I'm probably old enough to be your mother."

"How old do you think I am?" He chuckles.

"Early twenties?"

"I'm 40!" he tells me proudly. I can tell he's pleased by my response. He's clearly used to being told he looks young. He doesn't realize he has a stupid-looking baby face.

"How old are *you*?" he asks me.

"I'm 70" I say, thinking this is a clever little way of teasing that I'm too old for him. Surely, he'll realize this is my way of telling him I'm not interested.

Instead he says incredulously, "Really??? Wow! You look great!"

Oh my God! He really thinks I'm 70! Suddenly, I'm extremely depressed. Someone actually thinks I could be 70 years old! From now on I'll say 99 – no, better make that 210 – to make sure it's an obvious fib.

"No, not really. I'm kidding."

L-S Larry: "Oh. Well, these days you never know. I'm really bad about ages. So really, how old are you?"

Me: "I'm turning 48 in a couple of days."

Once again he's surprised and repeats in the same shocked voice, "Really??? You're only turning 40? You're younger than me?"

It's loud in the bar, and apparently, he didn't hear me quite right.

"No." Now I'm clearly annoyed. "I said I'm turning forty-EIGHT" I'm practically screaming across the chatter at the bar.

Heads turn.

At this point, I'm sure it's obvious, even to him, that I'm not enjoying this conversation. We quickly finish our drinks and say our goodbyes. He moves on, undoubtedly looking for some other willing vacationer to help him find where the alcohol is hidden in his room.

And me? I move over to the computer room. I miss Laptop Guy.

February 25 6am

I'm up early, out on the balcony, looking out over the ocean. It's gorgeous. I'm feeling melancholy and lonely. Today I'm going back home to cold Colorado. My vacation is almost over, the month is almost over, and my 47th year of life is almost over. Wait a minute....I do a quick mental check... Turning 48 means I'm at the end of my 48th year! Oh no. Another whole year lost in that calculating moment. Why do I have to be so good at riddles?

This goal to go out with a new man each month? I can't do it. I can't even find someone to kiss. I've failed my inner Devil.

Devil: Yeah, you had your chance with Leisure-Suit Larry. Stop moping, you whiner.

Angel: There are people all around to love, dear. In the spiritual sense, of course.

I have to admit, the thought that if I'd listened to the Devil, I might be waking up this morning next to Leisure-Suit Larry's baby face makes me certain that I made the right decision last night.

Whether I listen to the Devil or the Angel, they're both right in telling me to drop the pity party routine and take advantage of this last morning on the beach. I swallow that lump in my throat, close my eyes and enjoy the morning breeze.

February 25 11am

Jessica, Tom, and Rick, are playing in the ocean and yelling for me to join them. I work my way out, jumping the waves. They're riding them; I dive in, letting the waves carry me towards shore. I love the ocean. I once read in a writing book that the ocean should never be described as *turquoise.* It's too trite. But I'm breaking the rule. The ocean is what it is – incredible shades of turquoise.

I laugh and play with my new friends. We're still teasing one another.

"You are so gay, Alfred!" I taunt Rick. He's more serious than Tom, but he's having fun, too, showing us the *right* way to do this wave-diving activity. He tells us he's an expert and used to do it all the time as a kid.

"And I'm going to tell the world that you once were a girl, Tom!"

I promise them I'll change their names. Tom can be "Pat" (as appropriate for either a man or a woman) and Jessica can be "Grace", beautiful, classy, and naturally graceful. Despite his protests, I tell Rick I can only think of him as "Alfred" after calling him that all week.

I fill them in on my encounter with Leisure-Suit Larry and the missed opportunity for a Mr. February fling.

"Who wants to fill in? My first choice is Jessica."

They splash me. "I'm making you the most wet!" laughs Tom.

Suddenly, I see Rick zooming towards me! He's caught a big wave and I'm not able to avoid him. He's right on top of me, knocking me over in the ocean. We're both embarrassed for a second as we try and recover our places in the ocean.

"Sorry" says Rick.

I'm thinking.

I sort of just got *flung.* Yeah... I got *swept off my feet.* You could even say I *got laid.* I think I can work with this.

"I know what your name's going to be in my book, Rick."

"Don't write about me in your book!"

"Congratulations! I officially dub you: Mr. February" I say as I throw a big splash his way.

He dives after me, and I scream, trying to swim away.

He easily catches me and I'm laughing, swallowing water, thinking, "I'm gonna get dunked."

He's holding me as I struggle.

"Don't do it! Don't dunk me! I'm sorry. I'm sorry. I won't write about you, Alfred! I promise!" I giggle.

"Hey!" he says, "Stop your kicking." He's holding me tight around my middle. It feels kind of nice, though I'm aware that between his hold and the waves, my bathing suit is creeping places it's not supposed to creep. I do a quick check to make sure at least my boobs aren't falling out. I think he can touch the bottom of the ocean with his feet but I can't, and I'm still flailing.

"Wait for it," he says as he looks out seeing a wave rolling in.

"Now!" He dives in with me in tow, and we're carried toward the shore with the wave.

We emerge and I'm making a gaggling sound as I simultaneously scream and cough up the ocean. I wasn't expecting that. My face is devoid of makeup. I'm sure I must have eyes that are swollen and red from the salt water and snot that is streaming out of my nose as I work to catch my breath. Clearly, Grace is not a good name for *me*. I finally compose myself and look at Rick.

"Oh my God, Alfred! You rock my world!"

"Hey!"

He gives me his mock mad face. The one I'm used to by now.

"My name is *Mr. February* and don't you forget it!" He opens up his arms. I come in for the hug and then, surprise! He swoops his arms around in an arch, showering me with more ocean, totally cracking up at his prank!

February 25 2pm

I'm waiting on the hotel curb for the shuttle back to the airport. Jessica, Tom, and Rick have one more night at the resort. Goodbye, Grace. Goodbye, Pat. I look at Rick. "You're a pretty good game-player, after all, Alfred." Mock mad face. Open arms. I look at him suspiciously, but this time there's no ocean, so I trust him. He gives me a hug with a little extra squeeze to it.

"Goodbye, Mr. February."

He gives me a kiss on the cheek and then whispers in my ear, "Goodbye, Agnes."

February 26

Scotty's made me the most wonderful cake. I'd bought the mix and frosting, knowing he'd want to celebrate appropriately. Scotty *loves* cake. When Paul and I told him we were getting divorced, he said, "That's OK. I'll get to eat more cake." I was thinking he must be confused. People usually don't eat cake when divorcing. When I questioned him why he thought he'd get more cake he answered, "When you and Dad get married again." That's Scotty. Always the optimist.

So, of course, birthdays are always celebrated with cake. However, I'd neglected to buy candles. When you get to be 48, you figure you can do without the expense or fire hazard. Scotty hadn't let the lack of birthday candles prevent him from decorating this cake. He had somehow found every candle that would fit – tea lights, votive candles, tapered candles – to make me the most beautiful, unique, birthday cake I've ever had.

After reviewing these journals I am shocked by reading the February 24th entry. It's one thing to entertain the notion of a one-night-stand with a human, quite another to casually engage with foreign computers. That entry ended with Yvette opting to spend her evening in the hotel computer room. Those computadors...sitting out in the open, flaunting their accented keyboards, requiring payment for a mere 10 minutes of slow connection. Fingerprints on their dirty faces, their disks filled with viruses...most of them can't even get a site up anymore.   Is she that desperate for eMale?

March

March Goals

1. Adventure: Polar Plunge at Frozen Dead Guys Festival
2. Love: Date a Young Guy (??)
3. Write: Enter Writing Contest

Thanks to Google, *Match.com*, the World Wide Web and Laptop Guy, I have honed in on the specifics of my March Goals:

Adventure: Nederland Frozen Dead Guy Festival

Coffin races, hearse parades, masquerade balls, and a polar plunge, all celebrating the end of winter (yay!) and the "frozen dead guy", Grandpa Bredo. Apparently, the town is famous for this festival and people come from all over the world to participate. I read about the history in Wikipedia.

In 1989, a Norwegian *citizen named Trygve Bauge brought the corpse of his recently deceased grandfather, Bredo Morstøl, to the* United States. *The body was preserved on* dry ice *for the trip, and stored in* liquid nitrogen *at the Trans Time* cryonics *facility from 1990 to 1993.*

Now this kind of thing is right up my alley – dress up festival, end of winter, silliness – I love a good theme party. The Polar Plunge sounds like the perfect March adventure! I hate the cold, so what a good way to stretch myself and find something that will really be a challenge!

Mr. March

I haven't really been paying much attention to my *Match.com* suitors, but after doing a quick inventory of the people that have contacted me, there are two I like.

Josh is a sweet, 51-year-old widower. His flirtations are very innocent. Big problem with Josh: He lives in Virginia. He had emailed me in January, right before I went to Phoenix. He was going to be in Phoenix, too, but our schedules just missed each other. He was flying out the day I was flying in. I'd told him to carve me a message with his number on a tree, and if I found it, it was meant to be. He laughed and we've been emailing occasionally ever since. He says he'll be in Vail, skiing with his brother over Spring Break.

The other guy is a 31 year old never-been-married pilot. Photos look great. Smart, fun, handsome. He doesn't email very much so I don't know too much about him, but he's interested in going out.

Which guy would be better for Mr. March? Which one would be more of a risk?

After my pathetic lack of action in January and February, I'm ready to make up for lost time. I have to be more daring! I should try the "cougar" thing everyone's talking about. It's very trendy for younger men to date older woman. I guess I lucked out by being an old, single woman when it's in fashion, so I have to take advantage of this. And interestingly the words cougar and courage have almost the same letters! A sign? I'm trying to get over my insecurity about my age, and if nothing else, I'd say it's pretty daring to go out with someone 17 years my junior. Growwwl. (That's me, being a cougar.) I'm so proud of myself.

The young guy's name is Marc. It's another sign. Marc sounds like March.

Essay Contest: Most Embarrassing Date

Another stroke of luck! A writing contest sponsored by a local coach about the very thing I like to write about!

March 3

I'm going through a crisis. FB is on *Match.com*, too. He's been IM'ing almost every day, asking me a lot about online dating. I stupidly thought he was asking because he was jealous, but today he tells me that he signed up and he wants me to proof his profile before he makes it public. He suggests I might want to totally rewrite it for him because he's not good at this stuff. At first I think he's kidding about being on *Match.com* at all! He's the most introverted person I know and he's really bad at dating. So bad at romance that it's cute when he tries. He's a book-lover, not a womanizer. He has NEVER, in his whole life, been the pursuer. He makes fun of online dating! Not his style. He's the strong, silent type and women are attracted to that. God knows I am.

I know he will never love me. I've reminded myself of that a million times. The closest he ever came to telling me he loved me was the day he IM'ed me: ILYTTMAB. I Love You To The Moon And Back. It was probably just meant to be one of those acronyms that people use in IM and don't really mean like LOL. I mean how many times are people really *laughing out loud*? But still. It was an unprecedented, unprompted, spontaneous acronym that started with ILY so I've held on to that. It gave me hope. All this time, I don't think he's dated anyone else. I know he hasn't slept with anyone else. At least I'm pretty sure. He never needed to. He had his books, his independence, and sex with me whenever he wanted. My only condition was that he didn't sleep with anyone else.

Of course, he knows I'm on *Match.com* and actively pushing myself to *experience* other people. It's unreasonable for me to be jealous or upset that he would want to do that, too. I certainly can't expect him to become a monk. I'm just glad he warned me before I stumbled across his profile. I read it. I think I'm pretty close to what he describes: intelligent, honest, active. Why can't he love me? OK, so he wants someone that "is passionate about what's going on in the world." I know that's his way of saying he wants someone that is passionate about politics. He is obsessed with hating Bush. (The president, not pubic hair.) I'm a middle-of-the-road kind of person. I'm equally disenchanted with both the Republican and Democratic points of view and the more extreme someone is, the more I'm inclined to argue, even if I have no factual evidence to back up my claims. It's probably best for me to avoid political discussions all together, but unfortunately, that is one of FB's favorite topics. He actually believes the Bush administration is responsible for 9-11. I think it's good he didn't mention that in his profile.

FB's profile is relatively unoriginal. I comfort myself in thinking he won't get much interest. Then I come to the last line. It's different than any of the others I've read. It doesn't say "I'm looking for..." or "I want to find..." It's addressed to the reader. I don't know whether to be hurt that he's saying this to the entire *Match.com* female population or touched that he might mean it for me. I take it as the second since he asked me to read his profile first.

That lump in my throat is back.

"Your profile is perfect." I tell him. "I like the last line the best."

It reads:

"I hope you find someone who will love you to the moon and back."

I hope I do, too.

And I really hope I do it before you do.

March 8

I'm the kind of person that is naturally colder than everyone else. It's no coincidence that my first two adventures of the year included going to warm places. I'm trying to appreciate winter, but it's not working. This festival is fun but I hadn't realized how cold Nederland was. Boulder is cold, but Nederland is at a higher elevation and this is just about the coldest I've ever been in my life.

Some big men with chainsaws drill through the thick, icy Chipeta Park fishing pond. It's taking 30 long minutes. The sun is nowhere in sight, the wind is biting and I feel numb all over. The thermometer must read negative-something. Fire-fighters are standing by to quickly rush those that need emergency care to the hospital. I imagine the headlines: "Frozen Dead Girl Joins Grandpa Bredo in Icy Eternity." I would guess dying by voluntarily jumping into an icy pond, besides becoming an additional honored person at this festival, is also stupid enough to warrant a Darwin Award. It's CRAZY to jump in that pond.

That's why I'm SO glad I chickened out. Even bundled in my winter coat I'm frozen. There is no way I am EVER going to take the Polar Plunge. I don't think watching the Polar Plunge is much of a stretch, though. I'll just have to figure out a different March Adventure.

As I'm standing in the crowd with my friends, Chet, Jeannine, Zach, and Scott, I happen to glance over at the birch tree I'm standing next to. Someone has carved a heart with the message "I LOVE YOU" inside. It is so sweet and I feel like this tree is sending me a message from the universe. Maybe this is what it means to find love when you aren't looking. Maybe it's a sign that Josh, the sweet guy from Virginia should have been my Mr. March. He said he'd carve a message in a tree for me.

Angel: It's a message from God, Dear.

Devil: It just means you're so desperate for love that you'll accept hearing it from trees. That carving was meant for someone else,

Sister. Don't think you're gonna get out of your goals just because you happened to find a tree. You're already chickening out of jumping into a frozen pond. Don't chicken out on the date. Are you a Cougar or a scared little Pussy Cat?

I'm still moved by the unusual love note and I take a photo. It makes me happy. I'll send it to Josh and tell him I found his message.

March 9

I submitted my essay for the Most Embarrassing Date contest. My first overnight date with FB.

I totally exaggerated that story to make it funny. I was not really that gassy – maybe a little bloated – admittedly some fear of an unfortunately-timed fart, but it never happened.

Actually, that weekend, we had a whole ice-cream-sundae body thing going on before I even got the hint of a stomach rumble. Kind of sticky, but, for the record, I was very sexy. I just didn't write about that because I had to make it into a cute embarrassing date story for the contest.

Devil: I want erotica. Do you think you can spice up this journal a little? That date with Mr. March better be worth reading about.

Angel: Dear, I think you've said more than enough about sex. And talking about gas isn't much better.

March 10

I've figured out a new March Adventure. In hopes of sharing the experience, I've put out another mass email to all my *Rebuilder* friends. They've all been divorced. Many of them are in new relationships, so they don't all technically qualify as *single.* It doesn't matter, really. I'm not looking for a date—just someone to keep me company. I'm doing this when Josh will be in Colorado, so there's a possibility of meeting up with him, too.

On Mon, Mar 10 at 9:31 PM, Yvette Francino
<yvette.francino@gmail.com> **wrote:**

I know none of you will believe it, but I did not take the Polar Plunge at Nederland Frozen Dead Guy Days, so I am back,

41

coordinating another March adventure.

Sandy told me about this snowshoeing amongst the moose on the Spring Solstice, Mar 21, in Gould and I thought that would be a pretty cool adventure (well...it will probably be a cold adventure).

Here's my plan:

Friday day: I'm heading up to Walden where I'll be staying at the Antlers Inn. This is about 25 miles from Gould and includes a common living room area with a fireplace.

Moonlight Ski & Snowshoe Romp: This is scheduled from 4-9pm. It will be a full moon and the place will be lit up with glow sticks....sounds beautiful! There will be hot chocolate, cider, and brats. It will be very cold, though (-1 degrees last night). The trails are groomed and flat. It's a 6-mile loop. (By the way, I've only been snowshoeing once before. There's not too much skill involved.)

Feel free to invite others. Part of my adventure-of-the-month concept is to do fun, romantic things with myself....and whoever else happens to want to join me! :-)

Yvette

March 14 9pm
I'm into themes and word play. I'm throwing my daughter, Megan, an Alphabet-Themed Wedding Shower next month. She's very particular and as mother-of-the-bride, I'm trying to do all the right things. She really likes my Wedding Shower ideas so I have theme parties on the brain. Megan's party has nothing to do with Mar-words, other than it has put my brain into thinking about words with a common theme.

March, Marc, Margs. There are lots of Mar-words. I should see how many Mar-things I can do tonight at this bar I'm at tonight with Marc. Oh... I can have a Martini! Maybe I can ask Marc if he has any Marijuana on him. Not that I'd want to smoke it. It has a nauseating smell. It would purely be for the Mar-theme. I might even surprise myself and think it was simply Marvelous. I'm thinking of more Mar words while Marc is talking to the bartender. Maybe I should call him a "MARtender". If I had a Mar-party, I could tell people to dress like Martians and have Mars Bars as a snack. I could invite people named Mark, Mary, Marianne, Martin, Marti, Margie and even Marmer.

BTW, Marmer's alive. He sent me an email asking me about Mexico. Does he remember he totally blew me off? I called him to make sure I hadn't misjudged him. He was embarrassed and told me he'd gotten together with an old girlfriend right when we'd been discussing Mexico. On second thought, I don't think I'll invite Marmer to my Mar-party.

I don't think Marc will be amused by my Mar-theme so I don't mention it to him. I don't really want any marijuana-smoking going on. I'm trying to get drunk enough to follow through on my courageous cougar goal, but not so drunk as to act utterly foolish. The attempt at cougar behavior will satisfy the devil. The attempt to avoid foolish behavior is for the angel. I can hold my alcohol like a maritime man (I was going to say sailor, but...you know...still thinking about mar-stuff.) The bad thing about my high tolerance for alcohol is that I have to drink *a lot* to even feel a buzz. Tonight I'm not holding back. I am going to stage four. Drunk enough to have sex with a guy I hardly know, but not so drunk as to fall asleep and forget the whole experience. I figure it equates to approximately five drinks.

I have my sexiest underwear on underneath low-riding jeans and a tight cashmere sweater. Megan gave me a thumbs up on the jeans and sweater and told me I looked like a stylish Mom. I know she wouldn't hesitate to tell me if I looked like a middle-aged idiot. I didn't get her approval on the underwear, of course, and I do have my reservations about wearing panties befitting a whore on a second date. I also didn't mention to her that the guy I was going out with was a lot closer to her age than to mine. But I'm not going to think about age tonight!

Marc is very good-looking. Kind of like a young Tom Cruise. He's very happy-go-lucky. Likes his job. Flies a private plane for some rich guy. He says he hardly ever has to work. It sounds like he has very little responsibility, either professionally or personally, and he likes it that way. He's never had a long-term relationship. He likes to travel.

He says he likes older women. They know what they're doing. Uh oh. I wonder if I should let him know that I have absolutely no idea what I'm doing.

Finally. I'm going to be like a modern, sexually evolved, independent womarn. I'm like an unMARried norMARl woman. I'm prefectly mormal... I mean NORmal..but i'm tryhing dto stiiiick with the mmar theme....can't rwright..he wantes to goback to his amartpent. Marc is kissing my neck...mmmmm...i hope idont barrf..marrfff

March 14-15 Middle of the night some time
I don't remember too much about getting here, but we are now in Marc's apartment. It reminds me of the type of place you live in when you're in college only it's not decorated. There are no pictures on the walls. Crates are the main form of furniture. They are used for book cases, a TV stand and end tables. His one piece of fancy furniture, his new $2000 bike, is sitting in the middle of the living room. I can't believe someone that's over thirty lives here. Megan's house looks so much more put together than this place. Maybe that's because she's a twenty-three-year-old version of Martha (Another Mar-Name!) Stewart, so it may not be fair to compare the two. Even Matt's room at Berkeley looks more "mature" than this! It's too bad *immature* is not a mar word.

We sit on his couch – the type that usually comes with furnished apartments. He turns on the TV and starts channel surfing. He decides on his station and then starts kissing me. The kisses, up until this point, have been on the neck. I think. It could be I just didn't notice them, but now he's going for a long, French kiss. I haven't had a lot of sexual partners, but I've done my share of kissing, and this guy does not know what he's doing. Or maybe younger people kiss more aggressively these days. His tongue is jamming down my throat. There is only one sexual act that I know of that brings on the gagging reflex, and it isn't kissing. Not only is his tongue way too deep in my throat, but this kiss is lasting forever! I wonder if someone can become asphyxiated from a kiss. I keep trying to push his tongue away from my gagging-area with my tongue, but he isn't getting it. I think he thinks I'm enjoying this tongue-wrestling match and he's determined to win. I eventually just stop the tongue struggle and I manage to live through the kiss. I think perhaps I should explain to him that the phrase, "he takes my breath away" is just an expression and not to be taken literally. There is serious danger of me barfing while he's kissing me if this keeps up.

Now he's removing his pants and he has a G-string on! My God. Are there women that really get turned on by men wearing G-strings? Is this considered the new sexy style of underwear for men? First Marmer and now Marc? Maybe it's part of how the whole cougar experience is supposed to work. I think maybe I should just stick with old guys.

Marc impatiently pulls my sweater up over my head, attempting to remove it. It's kind of tight and gets stuck. My tummy and bra are showing and my face and arms are still covered with my inside-out sweater. I haven't practiced gracefully removing this sweater, and it appears something is not quite right. Is there some kind of zipper or something that needs to be undone? While I'm blindly struggling, trying to get my sweater off, he unhooks my bra-strap! Oh my God! Now I have both my sweater flailing around my head and my boobs loose around a dangling bra. The bra can't come entirely off, of course, because my arms are still caught in my sleeves.

At last I'm able to remove the tight sweater and the bra falls off with it and Marc's staring at my breasts. The lights are full power and I feel like I'm under a spotlight. I can't bare to imagine what a freak I must have looked like a second ago struggling with my sweater as my bra was hanging loose. I am totally self-conscious and tell him I'm not comfortable. He suggests moving into the bedroom. He asks if I'm on the pill. He doesn't like to wear condoms. Lovely. My friend, Brody (who likes to advise me on sexual matters) had prepared me with one of the super-duper-special-condoms from his stash, but it doesn't look like I'll be using that baby tonight. Secretly, I'm relieved. This might give me the out I need.

I try to figure out how I can tell him I've changed my mind about this whole encounter. Michael has trained me not to say "We are not going to have sex tonight." How about: "I meant to tell you I have herpes"? Better make that stronger. "I have HIV." I think these might work, but integrity, as well as my reputation, is important to me.

"I think the buzz has worn off" I say as I get up off the couch and out from under his dagger. I'm talking about his tongue, though I realize he has a bigger weapon with him. If his technique with tongue is any indication of his idea of foreplay, I really don't want to stick around for the main event.

"Would you like a drink?" he asks. "I have some beer."

"Um... No thanks. I don't drink beer. I think I'll just have some water."

I feel a little awkward talking to him while he's sitting there in his socks and G-string. I put my bra and sweater back on. I hope this makes it obvious that I want him to put his clothes back on, too. I go into the kitchen area to find a glass and help myself to some water. It's hard to find a clean glass. I just go into the bathroom and drink some water straight from the faucet.

Oh dear. There's a very bedraggled, tired looking person looking back at me in the mirror. My mascara is smeared and my eyes are red. I didn't even have any marijuana and I look like a stoner. What am I doing? Something must be wrong with me. There's a young, good-looking guy out there and I feel absolutely no lust. I just feel a lot of disgust. I have a tiny moment of enjoying that lust and disgust rhyme, even if they don't start with the letters MAR. Maybe some day I can write a poem about this experience. I look in the mirror again and resume my feelings of embarrassment and disgust with myself. I'm not a cougar. I'm just an old scaredy cat.

Angel: Don't say that, Dear. You're beautiful.
Devil: Bawk, bawk, bawk, bawk.

March 21

Zach, Sandy, and Allyson have responded to my email and want to do the snowshoeing adventure with me. Zach even offered to drive! Sandy and Allyson are meeting us up there. I'm so glad Zach's driving for two reasons: 1) I hate to drive. This is especially true when it's snowy and in the mountains. 2) I can almost pretend like this is a date!

Zach is definitely the most handsome of my men friends. I constantly tell him how cute he is and urge him to get out there in the dating world. I would love it if he got out there with me, but he says he's not ready to date—at all. He says when he *is* ready, he won't date anyone in the *Rebuilders* Community. Smart move. It can be a soap opera. I secretly think Zach just says this so desperate, middle-aged women won't hint around hoping to be asked out. I can't believe they can be so pathetic. No subtle hinting from me! I just overtly gush.

But since Zach has made clear that he is not in the market, I talk to him about all my adventures and *Match.com* experiences. I leave out some of the embarrassing details of the Marc date. I focus more on Josh, my new Mr. March. He's the guy that's out from Virginia who I'm meeting tomorrow in Hot Sulphur Springs.

"It's just a lunch. He'll be there with his brother. Why don't you join us?"

"No thanks."

"Allyson is coming."

"You and Allyson have fun."

March 21 8pm

This is magical! It's been snowing huge flakes—so fast and hard that we can hardly see anything but white flakes against black sky. There's a full moon out there somewhere, but the winter storm is hiding it. We have glow sticks to help us see, but the visibility is still limited. We look like snowshoeing snowmen.

I'm not even cold! I'm bundled up in my warmest gear. Nederland and Frozen Dead Guys helped prepare me to expect the worst. With my layers of clothing, I'm actually working up a sweat as we snowshoe through these snow-filled trails. No moose to be seen, but the mood is festive. Sandy, Allyson, and Zach are excellent Adventure-Buddies.

March 22 12 noon

Allyson and I are at the County Seat Grill in Hot Sulphur Springs. Josh and his brother, Mark (Another Mark! A sign!) walk in. Josh has short, gray hair and a sweet smile and twinkly eyes. A southern gentleman, through and through. We make small talk throughout lunch. I know from our most recent email exchange that Josh is looking for a practicing Christian. I've told him that I was raised Catholic, but lately I've been re-examining my faith. I haven't mentioned the influence the devil's been having on me. Since I've failed to follow-through on even the simplest sexual mission, I don't think it really fair to give the devil too much credit. Anyway, the standard rule when it comes to first dates is to avoid discussing religion, as well as sex or politics, so we just stick with standard small talk.

I like Josh. He's got a quality about him that I admire. Maybe that same spiritual faithfulness that I'd seen in Jessica, the woman I'd made friends with last month in Mexico. Josh is conservative and old-fashioned in mannerisms. He doesn't even own a digital camera. He likes his old 35mm. He's very sweet.

Angel: I really like this one, Dear!
Devil: Forget it, Sister! He's more conservative than you!

Surprisingly, I think the Devil is right. I never thought anyone could be too conservative for me, but I get the impression that Josh would be disappointed in my wild ways, not to mention my lack of Biblical knowledge.

Devil: What wild ways? Did I miss something?
Angel: I'm sure he'd be impressed by all those prayers you memorized in catechism class, Dear.

Sometimes I feel like a puritan goody-two-shoes because of my lack of experience, but with Josh, I can't even make my typical flirtatious innuendos without feeling like a floozy. He lives in Virginia, so I guess it's just as well that I'm not feeling like it's a perfect match. But I like him enough to hope we'll see each other again. I'll be going on a running adventure trip in Costa Rica next October and Josh says he may be interested in joining, too.

Allyson and Mark are being good sports as well on this blind-double-lunch-date. The men pay for the lunches and we give hugs goodbye. They're headed for the Denver Airport after a week of spring skiing. I tell Josh he's the best *Match.com* date I've had all year and that I'm proud to have him as my Mr. March. He asks if he can read my book.

"Some day, I tell him. "And thank you, again, for the note."

"What note?" He's confused.

"You know." I smile. "The one you carved for me in the tree."

"Oh that one! I'm glad you got it!"

I'm a lot younger, sexier, and sleeker than any of those men Yvette's been meeting. And my G-spot is clearly marked ta boot. Well, actually it's the ctrl+alt+del keys that are used ta boot. Those funky alternative key combinations, pressing multiple keys at the same time – it's enough to make my disk hum. And then sometimes we play these games – kinky stuff – she'll be the master I'll be the slave. Or she may plug in another device – an iPod or a digital camera – and watch as we're syncing. But, I shouldn't be writing about that. Who knows if younger devices like Blackberries might be reading?

April

April Goals
1. *Adventure: Host a Letter-Themed Wedding Shower*
2. *Love: Brody (?)*
3. *Write: Erma Bombeck Writing Workshop*

Brody stops by at about 4:30pm with a gift in hand. He plans on just leaving it on my doorstep, but I'm working at home today and I see him through my office window as he drives up in his sporty, refurbished Jaguar.

"What's this?" I'm not expecting either Brody or a gift.

"Just a little surprise," he says with a grin.

Brody and I have been friends for years. He's ten years older than me, though he could pass for my age thanks to his attention to cosmetic procedures. He proudly tells me Carly Simon's song, *"You're So Vain"* really is about him. He doesn't *probably think* it. He *knows* it. Brody has more confidence than anyone I've ever met. He's funny, smart, and rich. He's cute in a roguish way, always quick with a quip. Even though Brody's only 5'6", he says he's always the tallest in the room. It's one of the attitude mind-games he plays. I admire his confidence, but let's face it, he *is* pretty short. At barely 5'2", I'm vertically challenged myself, so I really have no business judging potential romantic partners on height, but I can't help it. We're attracted to who we're attracted to, and I like big guys. 6 feet, 200 pounds. That's how big FB is and that's the size I like.

Other than his height, I can't really think of any good reason why I'm not attracted to Brody. He's not too fat and not too thin – a good weight for his size. He's a good-looking guy and quite fit. And he makes me laugh. I guess we've just been friends for so long that it's hard to think of him any other way. Maybe it's time I start.

Brody has been paying a lot of attention to me lately and he's fun to hang around with. I'm tired of the chit chat of first dates. It's easy to talk to him about anything and he treats me well. Who else brings me a surprise gift for no reason?

"Do you want to come in while I open this?" I ask him.

"Sure," he says.

"I know what I'll do! I'll use that *Twenty Questions* game to see if it can figure out what this is." Last Christmas, Brody gave me this hand-held electronic game. It's this purple plastic device, about the size of a GameBoy, with flashing lights and a display – kind of a cheesy $20 toy in this age of computers, but the thing is simply amazing! (Laptop Guy is actually quite jealous of the little guy.) You think of an object and the device will ask you questions, starting with Animal, Mineral, Vegetable, or Other. There are buttons that let you answer: Yes, No, Sometimes, Maybe, and Probably. After twenty questions, the toy takes a guess at the object. The device must have some pretty sophisticated logic stored up in that little memory, because it almost always is right, even though some of the questions seem like it's completely off-track!

"I don't think it will be able to figure out what this is," says Brody.

"You'd be surprised! It's really amazing!" I tell him he's a very good gift-giver. "You always pick out the perfect thing for me. I hope this surprise gift is as good as my Twenty Questions Game!"

Brody doesn't want to play the game at first, but I talk him into it. I turn the device on, the little screen flashes, and the questions start.

Animal? No.
Vegetable? No.
Mineral? No.
Other? Yes.
The game counts that as one question.
Q2. Is it multi-colored? No.
Q3. Can it be used for recreation? Brody chuckles a little before answering this. No.
Q4. Is it heavier than a pound of butter? No.
Q5. Is it manufactured? Yes.
Q6. Can it be used more than once? No.
Q7. Can you smell it? Brody laughs at this one, too. Sometimes.
Q8. Can it fit in an envelope? Sometimes.
Q9. Was it used over 100 years ago? Unknown.
Q10. Can you eat it? No.
Q11. Do most people use this daily? Sometimes.
Q12. Do you carry it in your pocket? No.

Q13. Can it affect you? No.
Q14. Does it get wet? This one makes Brody laugh out loud. Yes.
Q15. Is it flat? Yes.
Q16. Does it come in different colors? No.
Q17. Could it be found in a classroom? No.
Q18. Would you find it in an office? No.
Q19. Can it be washed? No.
Q20. Does it help accomplish tasks? No.
And the answer is: Sanitary Napkins

"I don't believe it!" he says, impressed that the game got the answer.

"You got me sanitary napkins?" I don't believe it either. *What kind of weirdo gift is that?*

I open up the package and throw my head back and burst into giggles as soon as I can tell what it is. Bladder control napkins. The other night I'd revealed to Brody an embarrassing incident from my past when, laughing hysterically, I'd had a slight accident. It was hardly anything! Just a drip! Though it did happen at the inopportune time when I was in FB's bed. Brody went on and on about it as if I was incontinent. I tried to explain that women, particularly those of us that have had children, can have an occasional, very minor -I'm talkin' like barely a wet spot- accident now and then. I assured him this rarely occurs except perhaps while laughing uncontrollably in a very well-hydrated or inebriated state. Brody said that if we ever sleep together, he'd have to get a plastic mattress cover. I still think it's very common knowledge that most women have this pee issue – I even saw a *Friends* episode where Monica made reference to it. I can't believe Brody had never heard of this before. Men!

I'm a very good sport about Brody's little April Fool's surprise gift. I laugh some more and Brody suggests that we break open the bladder control napkins right now before I wet the couch. He thinks he's hilarious.

I throw the package at his face, but it simply bounces off his nose like a nurf ball. He's still laughing at his own prank and I'm wishing I'd thought of some embarrassing gag gift for him. Elevator shoes? No. Something worse. Extra-small-sized condoms . Next year....

I'm in Dayton, Ohio at the Erma Bombeck Humor Writer's Workshop, on the road to becoming a serious humorist. This conference is better than I could have hoped for. There are real writers here! People who have published books! I'm one of the few that has never had anything published. (I'm thinking a blog doesn't count.) And clearly I don't have the talent that these people do. In some of the sessions we do these little writing exercises. I sit there thinking the whole time, trying to come up with something witty. Most of the others are able to whip out clever answers immediately. I'm tempted to write them down and use these incredible off-the-cuff quips in my book, but I ask someone if that would be considered plagiarism and the answer is 'yes.' Darn it!

Devil: Chances are good no one's going to read your book, so get your notebook out and start plagiarizing, Baby.
Angel: Your poorly-written anecdotes are just fine, Dear. But do you think you could give me a better personality? Must I call you, "Dear" throughout this whole book?

Most of the sessions are about humor or memoir – the sort of thing Erma Bombeck wrote and the genre I'm shooting for with my *Laptop Dancer Diary* project. I'm very interested in this art of humor writing. I go back and look at my journals with a more critical eye. I try to rewrite parts, using humor techniques I've been learning, but the more I try and be funny, the less funny it is. It doesn't sound natural. In fact, it sounds stupid. I'm not dissuaded. I feel certain that I will be published some day. I am intelligent. I am confident. I am aware of self-publishing options.

April 5
Today in one of the small group sessions we're supposed to write and share an Erma Bombeck-like anecdote using some of the methods we've learned to incorporate humor and evoke an emotional response. Everyone gets out their pens and notebooks, quickly scribbling their ideas. These people seem to be able to whip out an essay in ten minutes and I can barely manage a sentence that I feel good about in that time. I have that Embarrassing Date essay tucked away in my writing folder. I make a feeble attempt at coming up with a

new idea, but everything that I start to write sounds so lame. Feeling like a kid that's cheating in school, I surreptitiously start copying my essay onto notebook paper, pretending like I can write on the fly like everyone else.

I was in love. I was a 43-year-old, newly divorced, petrified, exhilarated, infatuated, obsessive lunatic. I had fantasized for two months about my friend, FB, a 43-year-old single Dad, who had suddenly become the center of my every thought. Why had I never noticed what a Sex God he was? I finally got the courage to hint of my interest and to my intense delight, he asked me out.

Everything was going perfectly according to plan. Before long our first overnight at a romantic inn in the mountains was planned. I was ecstatic. There was one little problem. Somehow I had to transform myself from a middle-aged-Mom to a Sex Goddess in 2 weeks. After a crash diet and Victoria's Secret shopping spree, I felt a little more prepared. Experiments with lighting revealed exactly how dark the room would need to be to show off my sexy underwear, yet not reveal those unfortunate ripples on my upper thighs. As long as my push-up bra stayed on, I might be able to maintain an illusion of cleavage. My breasts had been through three children, all of whom I lovingly breastfed, little realizing that those suckers would ruin any chances of future strip shows.

The day finally arrives and I feel prepared. I've done my homework and have rehearsed for my debut as "Sex Goddess." We hike in the beautiful, romantic, winter wonderland. We flirt and hold hands. We dress for dinner and look gorgeous. I am feeling good! He wants me, I can tell. This is straight out of a romance novel. The dinner is delicious! I don't have to worry about that crash diet anymore. Suddenly, I have an outrageous appetite. I eat and eat and eat. Everything just tastes so good. We are both amazingly witty and the conversation gets more titillating as the wine continues to flow past our lips.

We head back to the room with great anticipation. Those butterflies in my stomach seem unusually active. So active, in fact, that they feel like they have now become attacking killer bees. The unique combination of my unusual eating habits, nerves, wine, and a tight skirt cause an alarmingly loud grumble to sound from my full belly. In one sitting, I seem to have gained twice the weight I lost on my crash diet. My plans for seductiveness never included popping the buttons off my skirt. I try to remain ladylike as I discreetly squelch my belches.

As I relieve the pressure by unbuttoning my skirt, FB takes his cue and moves in closer. The bees have now morphed into birds or lions or some kind of devil which makes noises that are getting progressively louder and more embarrassing. I panic. OH MY GOD! PLEASE, PLEASE, PLEASE, DON'T FART!

I politely excuse myself. The walls in the bathroom are way too thin. I run the faucets hoping the sound of running water will drown out any other "noises" that might emerge. The water is quiet and I am too embarrassed to risk releasing the enormous amount of gas that is apparently trapped in my body. So I sit on the toilet in a complete state of discomfort wondering if I can manage to redirect the gas towards my mouth and burp it out.

I get an idea. "I think I'll take a little bath" I sweetly say, refusing to admit the reality of my situation. The bath water is louder and I have hope of a slow underwater release that, if I'm lucky, will go unnoticed from the other side of the bathroom door. A valiant try, but I'm getting nowhere. I'm nauseous now, as well, and not sure which way I should use the toilet. In my efforts to be as quiet as possible, I spend what seems like an eternity in the bathroom.

When I emerge, looking anything but sexy, FB looks at me

with an amused expression and asks if I'm OK. "Not really", I say. "Maybe we should just try and get some sleep."

A few minutes later I hear another sound, only this time it's from him. Is that him snoring? Yikes! I decide instantly that I will never be able to marry him. Absence of a snoring partner is one of the few advantages of singleness that I'm not willing to give up. And, how dare he fall asleep rather than be lying awake restless and frustrated by his overwhelming desire for me.

Despite my disappointment at the foiled plans for romance, I take advantage of his snore-filled sleep to sneak back into the bathroom. Finally, by about 4am, I'm feeling relatively normal. I tiptoe back to bed, unsuccessfully trying not to wake FB. He asks again if I'm OK and puts his arms around me. I realize I am no Sex Goddess and he is no Sex God. And as I snuggle closer, I find I am more than satisfied just being a middle-aged-Mom in the arms of a middle-aged-Dad.

The woman next to me notices the type-written essay. She realizes I'm copying it. She must think that I'm copying someone else's writing! I want to tell her I've written it myself, but then she'll wonder why I'm not just reading from the type-written version rather than writing it over. Oh dear. What a tangled web we weave, once we practice to deceive. (Someone else wrote that. I'll look it up later and give appropriate credit.)

I decide to pass on reading my story when it's my turn. I don't want to risk being called either fraudulent or flatulent.

April 9

"Brody's going to be Mr. April," I tell Michael during our weekly Starbucks breakfast. "I'm tired of meeting new guys and Brody makes me laugh."

"Okaaay," says Michael in a skeptical tone.

"I know YOU think I'm settling, but I really like Brody, and height should definitely not be a show-stopper."

"Are you sure you're not being a little *short*-sighted?" Since Michael is 6'0" (and 200 pounds! just like FB) I'm sure he's feeling superior at the moment. He doesn't have to worry about anyone thinking *he's* too short.

"Didn't you tell me that Brody was a commitment-phobe? What makes you think Brody will even want to go out with you?" Michael asks.

"We already *go out*. We just don't do anything physically." Well, that's not *entirely* true. Sometimes, Brody grabs my hand or rubs my shoulders. He's kind of touchy-feely that way. Once, when we were playing tennis at his country club, I'd asked Brody if he'd pretend that I was his wife. We called each other "Honey" in that familiar fashion that married people do. Then we went to lunch and carried on the ruse. That night he'd sent me an email. "That was fun! Next time do you think we could pretend to be attracted to one another?" I reminded him we were pretending to be married, not in love.

"And he's funny. He gives really good email!" I like that line about "giving good email." In order to avoid getting sued by my friend, Sandy, though, I want to give her credit for using the line first when she was talking about our mutual friend, Charlie. Charlie gives good email, too. So does Michael, come to think of it.

Michael is not convinced that Brody and I are a good match. He thinks I'm in it for the money. That's Michael's hot button. Everyone has a hot button. Mine is age. Michael's is money. He thinks most women judge men on their cars and their jobs and their income. Michael has a good job, but his car is old and having lots of problems. He doesn't want to go on any dates until he has a better car. I think this is silly.

I don't consider myself a person who cares about status or income, but I admit, Brody's wealth is alluring. I could care less about his car, but I like the fact that when we go out he enjoys pampering me like a spoiled princess. Apparently, he also enjoys "Pampering" me like an old lady that can't hold her pee, but that's OK. Sense of humor is important to me. And now I'm equipped with bladder control napkins in the event of uncontrolled hilarity.

"Well, he's making me dinner Friday night, and he's very happy to be Mr. April."

April 11, 4:00pm

FB's told me he's going on a date tonight with someone he met from *Match.com*. He's nervous. I'm trying not to freak out. I've been on *Match* long enough to know that it never works out. But what if it's just that it never works out for *me?* What if FB finds someone immediately? Am I the only loser that can't find anyone? No, it's not just me. FB is picky like me. And he's a terrible dater. He'll feel uncomfortable and realize how lucky he had it with me. Yes, that's what will happen. Anyway, I'm going out with Brody tonight, and we're going to have a fabulous time. Brody gives me much more attention than FB ever did.

April 11, 8:00pm

I love Brody's house. It's this huge, white, Victorian sitting on a hill. Porches wrap all around the exterior and a quaint white picket fence surrounds his yard. This property reminds me of a full-size doll-house, completely furnished with just the right touches of romance. The massive yard is filled with gardens and big trees. It's all so beautiful and picturesque. Whenever I'm at his house, I feel like I'm visiting a Bed and Breakfast Inn. I love to sit on the porch and relax, just soaking it all in. Tonight Brody's made a scrumptious salmon on the grill, broccoli and baked potatoes.

Right now we're sitting in his hot-tub star-gazing and enjoying the stunning view of the Boulder city lights. Not to be immodest, but I'm looking very sexy in my new white crochet bathing suit. It's got this push-up bra thing going on enhancing my boobs to look better than they really are. Or maybe it's just 'cause I've had quite a bit of wine that I think my boobs look so good.

I can tell Brody likes my bathing suit and thinks my boobs look good, too. I deduce this when he tells me, "Your twins look good tonight. Can I play with 'em?" I could tell he was talking about my breasts because I don't have any twin babies and Brody thinks he's some kind of boob guru. He's played with my boobs in the past, but it's always been in Photo Shop. He says he's able to *enhance* photos, bringing out my best features. In one of the photos he's made me very voluptuous. In another, I'm triple-breasted. Though a bit unusual, the three breasts are very shapely, and strangely enticing! I've resisted posting them on *Match.com*.

Devil: I always liked Brody.
Angel: He sounds very dangerous, Dear. Are you sure you want to associate with him?

Brody's having fun playing the part of Mr. April tonight and this is a much better date than the March date with Marc. Brody's given me roses and is exaggerating the romance in a half-funny, half-serious way. He's one of my best flirt buddies and never fails to humor me with whatever game I'm playing. I know I'm one of many women he chases, just like he knows he's one of my many flirt buddies. The difference is that once Brody catches someone, he likes to sleep with his prey. Strike that. He doesn't sleep with them. He has sex with them. He tells me he never mixes sleep and sex.

I, on the other hand, have neither had sex nor slept with anyone this year. (Unless you count Laptop Guy.) Brody has been kind of like my sex coach. He is the friend that supplied me with that super-duper-deluxe-condom for my date with Marc. Thinking himself an expert, not just with boobs, but with anything related to sex, he claims he knows exactly what will turn a woman on. The first key is to understand the woman well enough to know what motivates her. Once he'd told me that if he were to seduce me, his first step would be to make a game out of it. I'd get points by performing certain foreplay actions such as a choreographed strip show set to the music from *Phantom of the Opera*. The actions would become increasingly difficult, in order to beat each level. The last level, gaining the most points and ultimately leading to a game win would be to engage in intercourse.

Obviously Brody knows me well. He's right that I'm gaga about games and will do just about anything to earn "points." Maybe I *could* make a game of this and try and seduce Brody.

Devil: I'd say your score is about -350 at the moment. Could you be any farther from him in that hot tub?
Angel: I disagree, Dear. Ten points for wearing that bathing suit that your boobs are falling out of.

I scoot closer to Brody and do a mental check on my lust meter. Zip! What is wrong with me?

I tell Brody about the disastrous date with Marc and let him know his super-duper condom is still a virgin.

"When you French kiss, is it supposed to be sexy to stick your tongue really deep down into someone's throat?"

"Absolutely not!" he assures me. "You want me to show you how it *should* be done?"

I just roll my eyes at him.

"Forget it, Brody. I'm never going to have sex again. I don't desire anyone! I had my chance with a young, hot, stud and I blew it!"

"You just need the right guy, Vetsky. Maybe a young, hot, stud isn't for you."

"Have *you* ever had the chance to have sex with someone gorgeous and not been the slightest bit interested?" I ask him.

"There was Ms. Georgia."

Brody often has *Match* meetings with out-of-staters. He either flies out to meet them or flies them to his place for the weekend. I think he fashions himself a younger version of Hugh Hefner. I'm amazed that these out-of-state rendezvous' usually work out well for him. No strings, no expectations and he remains friends with these women. I still hear tales of Ms. Utah, Ms. Florida, and Ms. California. Ms. Georgia is a new story.

Apparently, Brody had flown Ms. Georgia to Denver for the weekend. They roam around Denver with Brody doing his usual wining and dining thing. When they get back to his house, she wants to "freshen up." After awhile he comes down to find her. She's in his entertainment room, the one with the pool table and the big screen TV, and she's lying nude on his couch. (I think this may make a better story if she's lying on the pool table but I'll stick to relaying the story that Brody is telling me.) She proceeds to ask if he wants to see her "man in the boat." This, evidently, is a euphemism for asking if he wants to examine her clitoris. She spreads her legs, raised in a V, ready to give him a guided tour to her "boat" and the "man" within.

Brody is not prepared for this. Despite his wide range of experience in these matters, never had he so abruptly been thrust into this kind of surreal sexual scene. Ms. Georgia is confused by his lack of eagerness to explore. It seems that other men have jumped, literally, at such an opportunity. It does sound like something that only happens in porn movies, and I guess her body (I'm not sure if that would be considered her "dock") is playboy material. Brody said he found it all very clinical as he explored with his flashlight.

"I was thinking more men have probably gone down on this boat than the Titanic," he tells me.

Brody often claims he never ruins a good story with facts, so I'm skeptical of this whole account, but I'm finding it quite entertaining.

Brody says he was ready to drive her to the airport and get her on the next plane. Maybe most men would be surprised by this, but I understand completely. One thing I know about Brody is that he enjoys the chase, and he didn't get it with this one! No chase. No mystery. No anticipation. Just an examination of a man-in-the-boat. I think his story is hilarious and it makes me feel much better about the Marc March debacle.

"So how did you tell her you weren't going to have sex with her?" I want to know.

"I didn't say I didn't have sex with her! I said I wasn't *interested* in having sex with her."

"So *did* you have sex with her?"

"Well, I suppose it depends on the definition of sex, and who I'm talking to. When it comes to sex, I like to keep 'em guessing. That's the key, Vetsky. You might have the best 'man in the boat' around, but once you tell someone it's open for viewing, no one wants to see it. Keep it a mystery."

I assure Brody that my "man in the boat" is a rather private fellow and is not available for observation.

"We will probably never have sex," I tell him, "because I know you'd lose interest as soon as we did."

"*Probably* never? That means there's a chance we will. That's what I like to hear, Vetsky. Just keep a hint of *possibility* there."

I think, again, of the image of Ms. Georgia, with her legs spread, and Brody, tentatively peering into her crotch. It sends me into hysterics. Brody tells me to sober up and stop laughing. He doesn't want pee in his hot tub.

I recover from my bout of the giggles and close my eyes, leaning my head back, enjoying the beauty of the night. Brody turns me around and rubs my shoulders and back. It feels heavenly. I want to just enjoy his touch, but I can't. My mind starts to spin. I get nervous. This is feeling too intimate. I feel my body tense up. I turn back around and sit back on the hot tub seat. Brody moves closer and leans in to kiss me and I turn my head so that his lips hit my cheek. Awkward. I am such a dork! I adore Brody. Why can't I kiss him?

I'm embarrassed. Brody has been such a wonderful Mr. April, and I can't even kiss him. I've kissed dates I didn't even *like* before. As usual, Brody's cool. He laughs it off, teasing me that I'm giving him the longest chase of his life.

I'm glad he seems fine, but I suffer a wave of guilt, wondering if I've led him on. I suddenly have a flashback of my high school Prom. When I didn't want to give my date a kiss goodnight he got mad at me. "I spent all this money on you, and you can't even give me a kiss?" Is that how Brody feels? That settles it. I have verified that I am, indeed, defective when it comes to sex.

April 12

Though throwing a party may not seem like much of an adventure, it is definitely taking me out of my comfort zone.

The shower for Megan is on April 20. All the guests have been assigned a letter of the alphabet and I've asked them to be creative with their gifts, attire, and cards using their letter. I've assigned myself the letter 'Y'. When I was in Mexico, I'd bought a Yellow dress from the Yucatan to wear for the occasion. And I found the ideal gift -- a little bottle of Yves St. Laurent perfume called none other than 'Y'!

Now if only someone wanted to come to the party. Hardly any of my friends have RSVP'ed! Those that have responded seem very non-committal. Most of them aren't invited to the wedding. Megan had wanted to keep the guest list for the wedding limited to people she knew personally and hardly any of these women know Megan. But I want to have a party with my girl friends and share all this wedding excitement. I'd thought this shower was a great idea, but now I'm having my reservations.

My friends probably think it's insulting to be invited to a wedding shower when they don't know the bride and they aren't invited to the actual wedding. Or maybe they just think my letter-themed idea is weird and too much pressure – like I'm some kind of Kindergarten teacher giving them an assignment. I thought everyone would be so excited at my ingenious idea, but maybe they just think it's stupid and feel put on the spot. It's bad enough not having a boyfriend, but now even my girlfriends think I'm weird. Am I so off-the-wall that no one wants to associate with me?

I will try one more time to get those RSVPs. Being an Erma Bombeck Writer's Workshop graduate, I've crafted a clever little poem:

RSVPlea

Less than 2 weeks to go and I have a plea.
If you haven't yet done so, please RSVP.

If you're a "maybe" and there are quite a few
Perhaps you're in need of a party FAQ.

If I don't have a letter, you ask, will you yell?
Of course not. On your forehead I'll just draw an 'L'!

I don't want to play. Must I comply?
I assure you you'll want to and I'll tell you 'Y'.

When you're thirsty, you'll get to drink plenty of 'T'.
And then, right after that, you'll get to go 'P'.

The luckiest gal -- the one that's aglow
Will undoubtedly be the one enjoying the 'O'.

I don't know the bride. What can my gift 'B'?
Instead of the bride, why not give one to me?

All kidding aside, here's one thing that's true,
The thing we want most at this party is 'U'.

My house has been transformed into this romantic and whimsical fairy-tale setting! Megan is so good at this stuff. At first I was annoyed at her insistence on the colors – coral and turquoise. Does it really matter? My every day blue and gray are, apparently, "yesterday's colors." I hadn't really planned on redecorating my house to accommodate Megan's shower. But Megan had a lot of décor that she loaned me and we found a lot more accent – candles and vases and tablecloths of exactly the colors she wanted at – get this – the dollar store! And I found these faux pearl ornamental letters of the alphabet at Michaels! I can't imagine what anyone else would use these for, but they couldn't be more perfect as décor for an alphabet-themed-wedding shower! We've taken all this stuff, added lace and miniature lights in strategic places, candles of different heights and sizes, and it all looks ethereal!

And flowers – I don't know the names of all of them – I suppose if I'm going to be a prolific writer, I should pay attention to those things. I just bought a lot of different bunches that I thought might work. Whites and corals and purples. Lynn (Megan's future mother-in-law) is brilliant. She's able to do this magic with flowers. Mixing them and cutting them at different lengths, adding baby's breath and touches of this and that, creating gorgeous works of art.

The tables are beautifully arranged with each dish labeled: **A**ngel food to **Z**infandel. We've come up with a food or drink for every letter of the alphabet – even *X-rated mints*, look classy in my little crystal candy dish!

Now here's the part, if I were writing a fictional story, that I'd create some conflict. My friends wouldn't show up. Or maybe there'd be an embarrassing scene where the toilet clogs and overflows. Yeah, that would be a good one and quite realistic because my toilets are notorious for doing that. When we first moved to this house during the inspection, I told the guy about this problem and his response was, "Maybe you should add more fiber to your diet," as though it was the density of the poop that was causing the problem! Well, I'm sorry, but I am not going to tell all my guests they'd better be sure their stools are nice and loose before using my guest bathroom! In any case, there is no toilet catastrophe. There is no conflict. The RSVPlea must have worked, because the guests are here, their assignments complete. This is the best wedding shower ever!

The cards and the gifts are absolutely amazing. As each guest, presents her gift and reads her card, brimming with poetry and alliteration, I'm filled with so much admiration for these women. Even those from out of town that couldn't attend sent thoughtful cards and gifts, in keeping with their letter theme.

The poems, stories, and other creative uses of the assigned letter are funny, romantic, and touching. As I listen and watch these witty, intelligent, articulate women, I realize how lucky I am to have them in my life and my heart is so full of gratitude. How could I have doubted their friendship?

I'd like to fill this whole chapter with the creative work of these women. Most of them had given me a hard time about the "assignment," but when put up to the challenge, their creativity is worthy of its own anthology – "The A to Z Bride's Book of Love." Perhaps that will be my next project. But since I don't want to worry about the legalities and, this, after all is MY book, I will just include MY poem.

Words for the Y's

Yesterday You had Your Youth
Today's the day You Learn the Truth

The 25th letter of the alphabet
Is the Yuppiest Yummiest letter Yet

I'm sure You must be wondering "Y"
This rarely Yused letter rates so high.

"My Mom is partial" is what You're thinking I bet
"Of course she likes 'Y'. Her name is 'Yvette'!"

I'm not just Your mother, I'm still your advisor
Read more about "Y" and You'll find Yourself "Y"-ser

With Y as a starter, the words are quite few
But can You imagine having to say "I love ou"?

Y-words are Yuseful You'll find as a "Y"fe
Yawn, Yada, Yada, Ya know, Yeah right

Y also gives us great words of glee
Yay, Yahoo, You Go, and Yippee!

End words in a Y, and no one will Yell
Say Honey, Baby and all will be well.

The most beautiful Y-word for Chris I would guess
Must have been when he heard that lovely word, "YES!"

And last but not least, it's thanks to the Y
We have the chromosome that gives us the Guy.

Though sometimes they're clueless and hopelessly Yucky
To have Chris as my son-in-law, I feel incredibly lucky.
CongratYulations!

66

My Poem
by Laptop Guy

I was at the conference, too, ya know
I can spew out poetry like a pro.

I'm black and sexy with a big, hard drive
Better than any man alive.

Night and day, I'm always here
I don't ask for much. Not even beer.

You wear me out, but I've never complained
Except that night my battery drained.

Just plug me in and I'm full of juice
With all of that power I easily seduce.

With my high-speed memory, I won't forget
The secret desires and dreams of Yvette.

May

May Goals
1.   *Adventure: Mile High Amazing Race*
2.   *Love: Wedding*
3.   *Write: Journal*

Ah weddings. So romantic. So beautiful. So utterly, mind-bogglingly stressful. People tease me about being on the anal side when it comes to To Do lists, but compared to Megan, I'm a lightweight. She has lists for her lists. And she's a perfectionist. She's been living, talking, breathing this wedding for a year and half, involving most of the family members in the wedding preparations. It's as if we all have a part in a big Broadway production. Her cousin Rachele, is the assigned videographer. Her brother, Matt, will be the Emcee for the night. Lynn, Chris' Mom, is in charge of the flowers. Mark, Chris' Dad, will be officiating the ceremony. When it came time to hand out my part, Megan first suggested I make the cake.

"Have you seen the cakes I make, Megan?"

"But we took that cake decorating class, Mom!"

"And do you remember what my roses looked like? Those pathetic little blobs of frosting that didn't bear the slightest resemblance to roses? Trust me. You don't want me anywhere *near* your wedding cake!" I could see the wheels spinning in Megan's mind as she recollected my disastrous skills with cake decorating. Thank goodness she quickly reassigned that task to Chris' grandmother.

After further deliberation, I was assigned the duty of official Task Master. My orders are to keep Operation Wedding running smoothly. Megan has given everyone multi-page explicit instructions of exactly what they are to do and when they are to do it. I have been given the master plan. My only duty is to make sure that everyone else understands their instructions and are executing them to the letter. I'm quite confident that Megan, and all those to whom she has supplied her very thorough instructions, are fully able to execute everything and don't really need me. I have a hazy memory of a *Gilmore Girl's* episode where a clueless, bungling character was given the job of overseer of a project. The project had been completely under control and didn't need an overseer, but the task made the dummy feel important and kept him from doing any real work which he would inevitably mess up. I'm pretty sure that's why I got this job. I have no real skills to contribute. And though I'm relieved that this seems to be the easiest of all the wedding assignments, I've found I'm inept at handling even this.

For example, I'm supposed to check to make sure Lynn has ordered all the specified flowers. Since Lynn is a flower genius and I don't have a clue about Gypsophila Blossoms or Maiden Hair Ferns, I'm not even qualified to be the Task Master! Luckily, everyone else is very competent, so the thing I'm most worried about is Megan's stress level.

From: Meg <nervousbride@gmail.com>
To: Yvette Francino <yvette.francino@gmail.com>
Sent: Thursday, May 1 at 12:07PM
Subject: Wedding Nightmare

Hi mom, I have lots of stress nightmares about the wedding, but the one from last night was pretty funny so I thought I'd share!

First of all, everyone was wearing terrible clothes, like all the guys were way too casual, the bridesmaids were wearing blue, and you were wearing a white lace wedding dress with a veil!!!!!

Some girls I know that aren't invited to the wedding were there but they were so slutty, I could see through their dresses.

Also, I had some vows written down that I was holding, but I didn't know what was written and I was just going to read them anyway because I didn't even have time to read them before the wedding! Then the processional was starting and I didn't know where my bouquet was, I didn't even know what it looked like! So I crawled to the front of the ceremony hoping no one would see me so that I could ask Lynn where my bouquet was! She showed me where it was and then left, but it was not even flowers, it was like these stuffed animals only they were 3 stuffed hearts on stuffed sticks! They were really ugly! I was like "I'm not carrying that down the aisle" and freaking out, but you said that I should do it anyway so as not to offend Lynn!

Then they started playing Over the Rainbow as a processional song and someone was even singing it, it was terrible!

THEN Mark started the ceremony and he did the dorkiest thing!!! Because we have given him a list of how the ceremony will go, and the first thing on the list is a welcome speech, he just said "Welcome" and then he made a hand gesture of a huge check mark with a stupid grin on his face and everyone was like OK.....

But then, this next part was so sweet! I looked into Chris' eyes and he told me with his eyes that everything is OK, and I was so happy. I felt so much love for him. It was the sweetest ending to my nightmare!"

This email made me laugh out loud! I especially like the part where Chris' Dad, Mark, is making the hand gesture of a check mark after he welcomes everyone. Megan has given him his own checklist to follow, and I could just see him teasing her this way.

I tell Megan that I love the funny dream with its romantic ending and that I want to use the story in my book.

"Book? What book? What's it about?" I guess I haven't really talked much about my book with Megan.

"It's about love," I tell her. "Kind of like a mix of *Sex and the City* and *Chicken Soup for the Single Mother's Soul*. Your wedding dream is perfect because it's funny and has a sweet ending. It shows that you realize that what's really important is that you love Chris. None of the other details really matter." I'm hoping she'll remember that just in case I've inadvertently given the thumbs up to the wrong type of flower.

"That's great, Mom! What's the title?"

"I'm thinking of calling it *The Laptop Dancer Diaries*."

"Catchy! I like it!" Megan is very encouraging. She offers to be the illustrator and design artist and asks if she can read what I have so that she can start working on some sketches.

"It's in the very early stages." I tell her, suddenly coming to the realization that someday my family may be reading about my man-of-the-month fiascos. I tell her some of the stories are embarrassing and that I'm not taking it too seriously. "I'll probably just self-publish and check this off my life's To Do List."

"Mom, if you put your mind to it, this could be successful! The embarrassing stories are what will make it good. Don't leave anything out!"

I can't believe Megan actually thinks I can write a book that people will want to read! I'm not sure if it's because she believes I can write well or if it's just because she knows how embarrassing I can be. It doesn't matter. I'm totally flattered and inspired! Of course, this is the same girl that thought I could make a wedding cake. Megan seems to have supernatural abilities to achieve anything she sets her mind to, and I don't think she realizes that the rest of us are relatively untalented. But she believes in me! If Megan thinks I can do this, I'll do it! *Oprah*, here I come! Now I just have to sacrifice my dignity by continuing to create a love life full of embarrassing stories.

May 9

My family is very protective towards me and one of the ways they like to show this is to tell me that my ex-husband is a scumbag. While I secretly appreciate this loyalty, I remind them that we are all mature adults that need to treat each other with respect – in public, anyway. Since they will all be forced to socialize with not only Paul, but his wife, Trixy, I'm concerned about the brawl that might break out at the wedding. My strategy is to distract my family with a decoy. I've been on a mission to find the perfect date.

"I can't believe you didn't ask me!" I've just given Michael the sad tale of the stress I've gone through worrying about getting a date for Megan's wedding. I'd asked FB if he'd go with me over a year ago, when Megan had first gotten engaged. At the time, I'd felt sure he'd be my date, regardless of our relationship status. I figured he'd always be there for me at least as a friend. But, we're both moving on and I let him off the hook months ago. I'd considered various flirt buddies. Chet now has a girlfriend, so he's out. Brody's birthday is the wedding day and anyway, I still feel a little uncomfortable around him after the awkward ending to our April date. None of my *Match.com* guys are appropriate for wedding escorts. I had thought about going alone, but

I just couldn't endure looks of pity from my extended family and especially from Paul and Trixy! The poor, pathetic, ex-wife, unable to even get a date for her daughter's wedding.

"I did ask you," I remind Michael, "and you wanted to know if there'd be any hot, single, chicks there. Anyway, it doesn't matter because it turns out that my really handsome friend, Zach, is going with me."

Zach is adorable. He's got these dreamy blue eyes and classic good looks. Funny and smart, he could easily be cast as the leading male role in any romantic movie. Come to think of it, even though I'm not paying Zach, this plot is somewhat similar to *The Wedding Date* where Debra Messing hires Dermot Mulroney to be her escort at her sister's wedding. (Not to digress, but Dermot is an example of a name that does not go with a sexy person. Zach's as gorgeous as Dermot and he has a much better name.)

I'd been nervous about asking Zach if he'd go with me. I'm not exactly subtle about my admirations and he's politely, but firmly, been completely uninterested in a dating relationship. Zach has stated on many occasions that he's not ready to date anyone. Being "Mr. May" and my escort at this important family event is quite a lot of pressure for a guy that's not ready to date. Much to my surprise, he accepted my invitation!

"Yay! You know I've had to engineer this whole wedding scenario simply to finally get you on your first post-divorce date." I'd been teasing him for months that I could teach him all about dating if he'd just go out with me. I think it's a shame that someone as gorgeous and funny and, well, just the best catch EVER – feels he isn't ready for dating! But this all works out to my advantage because I get to be the lucky lady that will get to go on this first date of Zach's.

Michael seems a little offended that I referred to Zach as "my really handsome friend." "I can be good arm candy, too, ya know." He almost sounds jealous!

I assure Michael that he's also a very handsome friend, but that I didn't want my date to be checking out the hot, single chicks. Michael protests that I hadn't been clear that I'd been looking for a *date* and if I had, I'd be the only hot, single chick he'd be checking out. That's sweet. I guess Michael would have been a good choice, too. I'll remember that for the next wedding. But for now, I'm excited about going with Zach.

This morning, when I opened my front door, I found a beautiful bouquet of flowers in a big green vase on my doorstep. The card simply had my name on it and said "Somebody loves you." Could I have a secret-admirer? Today would have been my 24th Wedding Anniversary. Could it possibly be from my ex-husband? One of my kids? No one ever mentioned my anniversary before. Could I have a secret admirer?

Mystery solved. The flowers were from my friend, Craig. You may remember that Craig came to my rescue by providing male attention at the Kool in the Gang concert on my January date-of-the-month. Boy Toy Chet had invited two young ..ahem.. women, along and I needed to even out the male/female ratio.

Well, I recently sent Craig a care package and the flowers were his way of thanking me. In true "Craig-style" he sent me a funny email telling me that he'd taken on a new flower-delivery job and that he'd delivered a bouquet to my home this morning. "From the looks of that bouquet, someone must love you very much!" he wrote.

The email made me cry. I've been crying a lot. I haven't written about it because... well, this is supposed to be a humor book, and there's nothing funny about this. Craig was recently diagnosed with ALS – more commonly known as Lou Gehrig's disease.

I've been thinking a lot about faith. How could someone so devout, so loving – so "Craig" – how could someone that epitomizes goodness be stricken with this disease? He's 47 with three kids. I can't bear to imagine this world without him. I question God, unable to understand why this is happening.

But Craig doesn't question for a minute. His faith remains stronger than ever. He tells me he's not afraid. He wrote in his email telling of his prognosis:

"I especially appreciate the opportunity to show my children how life can be lived without anger, resentment, bitterness or regrets. I have purged all of that from my life and intend to leave this life with nothing but love, acceptance, forgiveness and compassion in my heart. I

am so ready to live life to its fullest. I only wish I would have thought to do it sooner."

I have so much admiration and respect for this man. I wish I could experience half the devotion and faith that he has. His courage inspires me more than words can say.

Craig doesn't spend a minute feeling sorry for himself. I cry at the thought of losing him and realize that that is the last thing he'd want me to do. He would want me to follow his example, love God, and "live life to the fullest."

From this day forward, whenever my faith is shaken; whenever I'm feeling sorry for myself or feeling angry at life's little injustices, I will think of Craig and remember his amazing attitude.

God, I don't get it, but I will try to be more like Craig and hold off on the questions. Just please fill the rest of Craig's life with love and happiness and give him a special place in Heaven when he gets there. I'm sure You know, there's no one that deserves it more.

May 16

The wedding has been such a focus, that I almost skipped a "May Adventure." I just didn't know if I'd have time. But this afternoon my friends, Chet, Wanda, and Marie, are running with me through the streets of Denver, solving puzzles and racing against the clock. We call ourselves "Four Play" (a brilliant team name that Wanda came up with.) We're in the Mile High Amazing Race.

There's a scavenger hunt and we're doing crazy things like collecting coins from everyone we meet, acting out improv at the Bovine Theater, and selling hot dogs at Washington Park. Chet even shaved his head at one of the stations! It's worth 15,000 points in this game.

Our team of four is versatile. Thank goodness the others know where we're going. When I'm on my own, I have the uncanny knack of going exactly the wrong direction in just about every navigational situation. (My GPS is often telling me to "Make a U-Turn" in a very condescending tone which I find quite annoying. Despite this, I've left strict instructions for the kids to pack the thing in my coffin, because I'm certain to head the wrong way to the afterlife without it.) In this race, I trust my teammates to get us from destination point to destination point while I focus on finding the odd items required for the scavenger hunt.

Not only is this an incredibly fun race, a big bonus is that it supports the Leukemia and Lymphoma Society. I originally wrote a big long passage here – a very heart-warming story about my first marathon and the fund-raising I did for Leukemia and Lymphoma. My Mom read it and told me it was the kind of thing that makes people want to stick their finger in their throat because it's so syrupy sweet. I'd asked for her constructive criticism, even though I didn't think she could really be impartial.

"You know, it's like when someone says, 'Gag me,'" she explains, sticking her finger in her mouth repetitively.

"I get it, Mom."

Seeing my mother doing the finger-down-the-throat-thing, was an eye-opener. Not only was it strange to see my mother performing an act that I normally would associate with a teenager from the 70's, she's usually my biggest fan. If *she* thinks this stuff is boring, I'm in big trouble.

So, I ended up having to edit a lot of this chapter taking out all the 'Gag me' parts. I don't think I got all of them. It's the sappy *Chicken Soup for the Mother's Soul* portion of the book. If you don't like that kind of stuff, feel free to skip to June.

Angel: This is my favorite chapter.

Devil: What am I even doing here? I did not sign up to be in any "Chicken Soup" chapters. Call me when you get to the sex scenes.

May 22

Four trips to the airport in the last two days, and the gang is all here. This is the first time Mom, Dad, Michele, Neal and I have been together for over two years. It always seems weird when we have a big family get together that Chris isn't here. My brother died in a car accident in 1997. Even though it's been almost eleven years, I still sometimes feel shocked to realize he's gone. It's kind of fitting that tomorrow we'll have another Chris joining the family.

My older son, Matt, is home from Berkeley, too, and Michele's two daughter's Rachele and Rebecca are here. It's a full house and I love the family chaos! But tonight we're heading over to the rehearsal and garden party and I'm nervous. Zach won't be accompanying me to these so I'll have to face my ex-husband and all his family on my own. Well, not entirely on my own. My family will all be there, too, of course, but, again, since the divorce they are not exactly Paul's biggest fans. I've given everyone strict instructions to be on their best behavior.

May 22 7:00pm

It's really very difficult to know how to socialize with Paul and Trixy. This may be why we have become so skilled at avoiding each other entirely. On those rare occasions, like today, when we are thrown into a social situation, we smile very amicably and pretend like we're all friends. My family is being very polite and friendly just as I'd asked them to be. Geez. They're even chatting and smiling as though they're having a good time. They don't really need to be *that* nice!

I know they're taking their cue from me, and as usual I'm being a responsible adult. If I were being "authentic" I would be much more likely to behave as if I were on one of those trashy talk shows like *Geraldo* or *Jerry Springer* and create a scene. Right now, at this lovely garden party, I'd take the flowers from the vases and throw the leftover water into Trixy's face! I'd say, "Yo Bitch! You and Me! Right here, right now!" and then I'd take Trixy down. After that, I'd smash the vase on Paul's head. My family would all be on the sidelines cheering, "You go, Yvette!" making those "hoo, hoo" calls as they punch their fists into the air at my victory.

That's all. Then I'd have it out of my system. Just five to ten minutes of low-class behavior. Is that too much to ask for?

Devil: You really should learn to swear before you have any more fantasies about being a trashy Beeoch.
Angel: What's a Beeoch?

May 23 4pm

"So am I supposed to be the *boyfriend* or a *friend*?" Zach asks as he's driving me up to the wedding site – a spectacular Victorian estate with a fabulous view of the Rocky Mountains. Zach's not sure how Mr. May is supposed to act, especially when meeting many family members including my ex-husband and my ex-husband's wife.

"My family knows you're just a friend, but I won't mind at all if you act like a boyfriend, especially around Paul." I tell Zach that he should feel free to have a public make out session with me any time the mood hits, except for possibly during the wedding vows portion of the program. Everyone will be watching Meg and Chris at that point and I want to be sure any and all displays of affection from Zach are getting maximum attention.

He looks exceedingly handsome. His tie matches the exact shade of purple of my dress. I'm looking quite exceptional myself, today. We almost look like Barbie and Ken dolls. Only Zach doesn't look gay, like Ken. OK, I don't look much like Barbie, either. But our clothes are very stylish.

May 23 4-6pm

This entry used to have a bunch of stuff about getting ready for the wedding. Megan looks like one of those models you see in photo frames – she's so beautiful that it's hard to believe she's a real person. Matt, Scotty, and my extended family are also extremely good-looking. Luckily, we have it all on video, since I decided to cut the flowery descriptions and blow-by-blow account of stringing beads through my daughter's long locks. The only part of this entry that was pertinent to this story line is a mildly entertaining anecdote when I trick Zach into marrying me, using his signature on the marriage certificate. Everyone *thinks* I was kidding, but when this book comes out it will be revealed that the paperwork will show it wasn't Megan and Chris that got married this day, but me and Zach! <Insert psycho-lady, evil laugh here.>

May 23 6:15 pm

At last, the processional hymn begins. The wedding party is lined up on the second story. We walk out, and descend, two by two down the romantic stone steps along the side of the estate, leading down to the garden where the guests are all seated. Matt is my partner, guiding me down the stairs and to my seat in the front row. My dress is slightly too long and my heels are high. I'm thinking that tripping and falling down the stairs would provide a funny story for this chapter, but I'm not willing to make that sacrifice, even for the book or the $10,000 I might win on *Americas Funniest Home Videos*.

The ceremony continues flawlessly. Everything – from toddler, Ava, spreading her rose petals, to the poignant vows that bring tears to our eyes – all carried off without a hitch. Nothin! I got nothin' to make this story more interesting.

Maybe there will be some drama when Paul and Zach meet.

Zach is charming. Cordial, but not overly-friendly. Hoping to create a little tension, I manage to throw in a comment about the "Big Game," wanting to let Paul know that Zach went to Stanford. Being a Berkeley Grad, I know this will simultaneously annoy and impress Paul. Maybe he'll challenge Zach to meet behind the trellis and duke it out? Nope. They just chat a bit and then Zach grabs my hand and suggests we go sit down. I love the way he takes my hand – so natural, without the slightest bit of uneasiness. Zach sensually glides his hand on the small of my back, guiding me through the crowd. (I added that "sensually" adjective just to give a little zest to this part.)

Devil: It's not working at all.

My heart is so full of emotion on this magical day. Fortunately for you, I will soon be deleting the several pages in which the "gag-me" factor continues to be way too high. I wish I had the talent to be able to grab these emotions, bundle them, and spill them out on paper, so that when you read them you'd feel how I feel. Your eyes would have tears welling just below the surface, your cheeks would feel flushed and your heart would feel ready to burst with pride and gratefulness and happiness. Of course, no matter how much I use the thesaurus to try to describe how incredible my family is, you readers are not going to experience this feeling. This is *my* family. So think of *your* family. Think about how much you love them until you get that "I will never, ever take them for granted" feeling. Think about it until you have those tears in your eyes. That's the feeling. If only we could bottle it up. The ability to capture love – I'd written about that in my blog, the day that Megan was engaged.

Love Dust

It's New Year's morning and my daughter and her boyfriend stop by my house unexpectedly, a look of excitement on their faces. Megan holds out her hand and shows me her new diamond ring. They are giddy with love, wanting to tell me the details of the proposal and plans for the wedding that she's been imagining for the past five years.

I see their excitement and wish somehow I could capture their feelings... love dust stored in a bottle, to be sprinkled whenever times are hard. I want Megan to remember exactly how she feels as they look at each other with playful happiness. They are naive and young, blissfully ignorant of the challenges that marriage can bring.

"Love dust? We'll never need that! Our love will always be this strong!" Megan would think to herself.

Little does she know.

There will be the times when he'll repeat that same story to every new acquaintance. It was so entertaining when she'd first heard it and she'd encouraged him to tell the story again and again. But by year ten, the story will have become increasingly exaggerated and she'll roll her eyes, thinking, "When did he become so full of shit?" Time for a little love dust.

There will be an Anniversary when she's exhausted yet still finds time to make a surprise romantic dinner only to learn that he's gone out with the guys. He'll come home tipsy, thinking sex will make things all better, not realizing that the only thing that can make things better is to relive that day where instead he comes home and showers her with praise and attention, claiming he'd never tasted anything quite so delicious. She won't be able to go back in time, but she'd have the love dust and that would make it better.

There will be days she feels overwhelmed by responsibilities, convinced that she does 99% of the work, taking care of the kids, the house, her job, the pets, and he can't even bother to pick up his dirty shorts? And what is that smell? She thinks maybe she could have her own room and they could just use the bedroom for romantic encounters. It's not like they don't love each other, it's just that she needs her girly space! She could sprinkle a little love dust around the room on those occasions.

There will be a time she finds herself attracted to someone else, knowing she'd never, ever cheat, but enjoying his attention. She'd dress a little nicer and check the mirror more often and feel a thrill when he laughs at her jokes. Then she'll see her husband enjoying a similar relationship with another woman and be very tempted to claw that bitch's eyes out. She'd need the love dust then, though she might be reluctant to use it, afraid that it might work on the wrong person!

There will be days she is angry and disenchanted, thinking life would be so much easier if she didn't have to constantly compromise. She'll remember her parents' divorce, barely a harsh word spoken, not knowing the devastating heartache from which she was sheltered. She'll think, "Divorce is not so bad. It happens all the time, and everyone is just fine." Those are the days I'd want her to sprinkle on a heap of the love dust, realizing divorce is, in fact, "so bad." Love dust is such a better remedy when there are problems.

On her 50th Anniversary, when she's dancing with her husband, she'll think of all the times over the years when she needed her dust. She may want to check her bottle, wondering if it's almost empty. She'll be surprised to find that, in fact, the bottle is overflowing, for every time the dust was used, it came back ten-fold, unbeknownst to her.

As I sort through my memorabilia, three years post-divorce, I find a dried rose, given to me by Megan's father many years ago. I toy with the idea of grinding it and bottling it as her love dust, but I realize it wouldn't be her dust, but mine. I find that even my love dust has power...not to eliminate grief and sadness, but to remind me that my love was real. I struggle to decide whether or not to part with my love dust, not wanting to let go of the little I have. Then I look at my daughter and her brothers and I know I don't need the rose. I've been blessed with an infinite amount of precious love dust. I wish her the same.

I made the mistake of telling Megan this essay was an engagement present, thinking I was passing along such great motherly wisdom. Though she didn't want to hurt my feelings, she told me the story was about me, not her, and that history would not repeat itself. She's in fairy-tale love and doesn't want it to be ruined by talk of the difficulties of marriage. I realize now she was right. It wasn't the right time. All marriages have their issues, but it would have been a lot better for me to just have given them something more traditional for an engagement present, like a framed photo or a popcorn popper.

May 23 8pm
It's time for the toasts. Paul is on the list for a father-of-the-bride toast. I feel a little irked that he gets to make a toast and I don't when I've been the more involved parent, but I understand. It's tradition. Paul takes the mike and gets up in the middle of the ballroom so he can deliver this oratory wonder. He pauses and makes sure the room quiets before he begins. "Marriage can either be Disneyworld or a trip to the dentist office." (I'm guessing Trixy is supposed to be Disneyworld and I'm supposed to be the dentist office.) "And the difference between 'It's a Small World' and 'rinse & spit' is whether you inspire each other or demand from each other." He pauses for effect. Then he goes on to some other really confusing metaphors. There's something about "calling marriage a commitment

81

is like calling a rabid pit bull opinionated." I resist rolling my eyes. Though Paul repeated to claim, "I know what you're thinking," I'm pretty sure he didn't realize that many of us were thinking, 'Huh????' This speech is going on and on about stuff that doesn't even have to do with Meg and Chris. He's talking about his parents and the hardships they endured. I look across the table at my sister, Michele, and we share a WTF look and then resist an urge to giggle at our shared expressions. This is probably the only part of the wedding that Megan hasn't scripted and I'm sure she's regretting it.

There's a lot about Paul that I admire and respect. He's a very intelligent man and I loved him for over twenty years. I have so many happy memories of our marriage. But this speech really sucks. It's nice that Paul is able to take the hit and provide the embarrassing story for this chapter. I realize as I'm listening to his long speech that I'm no longer angry or hurt that we're divorced. I'm relieved! Trixy will have to be the one to dig out the love dust on this one. A giant weight has lifted from my shoulders! It's not necessary for me to have a Jerry Springer fantasy to feel validated!

After several minutes of this speech, which includes recollections of Megan's stubbornness from the time she was a baby through her difficult teen years, my feelings of validation turn to fears that Megan's perfect wedding is being ruined. As Wedding Task Master, I should be putting an end to this! No one brought the big hook, so we could pull Paul off stage. Should I get his attention and tap on my watch? Or maybe clink my champagne glass?

"Hello, Everyone! Official Task Master here. Sorry to interrupt, Paul, but according to the wedding agenda, your time was up 10 minutes ago. Everyone raise your glasses to the bride and groom! Oh, and by the way, I just want you all to know that I'm here at this wedding with my handsome escort, Zach. I'm no longer married to Paul—the guy that just gave that terrible speech."

As it turns out, Paul finally wraps up his speech without a demand of 'rinse & spit' from his ex-wife.

As annoyed as I am with Paul's speech, I also feel a certain sympathy for him. Communication between he and Megan has been strained for many years. I'm sure he wanted this chance to say something meaningful. I'd heard later that he'd spent 3 hours in the library preparing. I realize that even he must suffer from bouts of insecurity and is probably just looking for love and acceptance from his daughter. In his own obscure way, I think he was trying to tell Megan and Chris the same thing I was with my Love Dust story – marriage isn't easy.

I doubt Paul will ever read *The Laptop Dancer Diaries* but if he does, I hope he can laugh along with me at the funny, stupid mistakes we've made. Whether we were at Disney World or at a dentist office, we always loved our children, and somehow we managed to raise three incredible human beings. Megan and Chris are bound to experience hard times in their marriage. It's inevitable. But for now, they are enjoying the magic of Love Dust, Disney World, or whatever you want to call it, and that's exactly as it should be.

May 23 10pm

Louie Armstrong is singing "What a Wonderful World" and Zach asks me to dance. I lay my head on his shoulder. Maybe it's the champagne that I've been drinking that makes me feel so sentimental. But I know that at this moment, I'm happy, here dancing with Zach – my sweet, handsome friend – my Prince Charming. This is my night to live in a fairy tale, and I'm enjoying every minute.

And I think to myself .....what a wonderful world.

May 23 Midnight

The bride and groom have ridden off in their limo. After loading all the gifts and decorations, Zach has driven me home. I could have ridden home with the others, but I want this night to have a proper ending. Zach has been everything I could have hoped for and more. My family was totally enamored with him, just as I knew they would be. He has played the role of wedding escort more perfectly than if I had written him a script to follow. I think anyone else would have been awkward in such a position. To be honest, I thought Zach would be awkward, but if he was uncomfortable, it didn't show. He seemed totally at ease. Even now, the end of the big "date", the old kiss-or-no kiss dilemma, and he isn't acting nervous.

Zach knows I adore him. I think of him sort of in the same way as a movie star. A nice fantasy, but certainly not a reality. A lot of men would not want to be put up on such a pedestal and certainly wouldn't want to play "wedding date" with someone they weren't really interested in. But Zach spent this whole evening being exactly who I needed him to be. Despite his qualms about dating, he was my wonderful Mr. May – my dream date.

I risk overstepping boundaries and ask if we can end the date properly.

Zach bends down and gives me a kiss. Like everything else, it's perfect. More than a simple peck of a friend but less than an intimate kiss of a boyfriend. An overwhelming feeling of love fills me as this magical night comes to an end. I'm so grateful for what Zach's given me. I know it was just for one night, but tonight was my fairy tale. I give him a hug goodbye and savor the moment. Goodnight, Sweet Prince.

Angel: What a sweet story, Dear. And you will live happily ever after.

Devil: Puh-lease! Kill me now.

Do you know where I was during all this family celebration? Packed away in a computer bag and stored in a closet! Not just unplugged. Not even allowed to sleep. I was completely stripped of my power. It was the biggest turn off ever! Talk about a Cinderella story! I was the one that was left home from the ball! I heard there was another Laptop at the wedding that controlled all the music. She could mix it up, her hard disk filled with music from all eras. If I had been there, she and I could have shared music files. Maybe even hooked up. I would have "accidentally" left my cable behind as we rushed home at midnight and she would have found me again. But noooooooooo.

June

June Goals
1. *Adventure: Manitou Springs*
2. *Love: Hmmm*
3. *Write: Journal*

"There are the kissing camels!" I tell my sons, Matt and Scotty, pointing out the classic rock formation at Garden of the Gods Park. We take lots of photos, not only of the kissing camels, but of all kinds of formations. This place is a veritable photographer's paradise. Garden of the Gods is a fitting name! We've been enjoying a Manitou Springs getaway with a little of everything – hiking, eating, and seeing all the local sites. Earlier today we sampled the five different varieties of natural mineral spring water around town. We'd heard the water has medicinal qualities. Personally, I had to keep from gagging – the taste was sort of like the water equivalent of curdled milk – which is why I only took tiny sips. I'm counting on that being enough to prolong my life until I'm one hundred and one.

I'm on my June Adventure. I knew I'd wanted to share it with the boys but I'd had a hard time figuring out what we could do. They enjoy these extreme things with their Dad – back country snowboarding, mountain biking in Moab, igloo camping in the Rockies. Most of the stuff they do, I'm just not physically able to master. Do you know it takes about five hours of cutting out ice blocks to build a personal igloo? I get tired shoveling my driveway! There is no way I could build an igloo. And I'm not shedding any tears over that because the thought of sleeping in one sounds about as appealing as sleeping in a refrigerator. No thanks!

"We could climb Pikes Peak." I suggest.

"We've already climbed a lot of 14'ers with Dad, Mom." Scotty says in a "been there, done that" voice.

"What kind of adventure do you want to have with me?" I ask, trying not to sound frustrated.

"How about we have a movie and game marathon?" Scotty suggests.

86

This does sound mildly appealing to me, but since Scotty and Matt have been doing that almost every night lately, it really doesn't sound like much of an adventure.

"We have to get out and hike or explore and do something different and memorable."

"I really like to relax," Scotty assures me. "This is the relaxing house." I feel a moment of irritation at Paul for wearing out my sons with all *his* adventures so they have no energy left for me.

"I don't want to just stay home and watch movies and play games! When you get old, all your memories and pictures will be stuff you did with Dad and all you'll remember about me is that I had the 'relaxing house'."

"You make good cookies, Mom! We'll remember that," Matt assures me. Normally I would be flattered by this, but the fact is, the "good cookies" he's referring to – the ones my kids rave most about – are just the Nestle Tollhouse type where the batter is already pre-made and all I have to do is pull apart the little square pieces and stick them in the oven. My kids are extremely generous with their praise of my cooking skills. A couple of years ago Scotty bragged to a friend's mother about what great spaghetti sauce I make. Apparently, he didn't realize that heating Prego up in the microwave isn't really considered *cooking* in most circles.

We finally agreed on this Manitou Springs getaway as the June Adventure and the three of us have been having an awesome time. We're staying in this huge, gorgeous condo, secluded in the woods amongst flowers and trees. Much more comfortable than any igloo. We packed a big stack of board games to play and plenty of food – stuff that I can cook really well, like pre-made lasagna and my famous Nestle Tollhouse pull-apart cookies.

June 1 8:00pm

My kids are all very smart and huge gamers. You'd think, Scotty, being only 13, would have a disadvantage when playing games with adults. But no. He's the best game-player ever, especially on strategy games. He'll beat me every time. But now we're not playing a strategic game – this is the type that has trivia questions and word puzzles. Scotty can still hold his own, especially on the science questions.

87

"Is there life on other planets?"

Scotty, in a very confident, authoritative voice answers, "No. Life does *not* exist on other planets because there are no orgasms on other planets." Matt and I burst out laughing and Scotty quickly realizes his mistake. "Organisms! I meant to say organisms!"

We can't stop laughing and suddenly anything any of us say is funny. It's kind of like when you're drunk and you think everything is hilarious, except we're not drunk. We're just in this silly mood. Maybe it's that mineral water. Laughter equals longevity. The magic medicinal power must be that the water makes you laugh at everything. (I later learned that mineral water can contain lithium. It's all making sense now.) This is the most fun, relaxing weekend I've had in a long time – just the three of us.

I feel a little bit of guilt for not attempting a more physically enduring June Adventure. Maybe the "stretch" this month, was accepting that my children do not expect the same kind of "adventure" from me as they get from their father. The memories they have of me are not going to be based on the risks we took, but on the time we spent together, whether that time was spent climbing mountains or playing board games. I comfort myself in knowing that we hiked many miles, saw breath-taking sights, and have just spent the last half hour laughing. And on top of all that, I made the best cookies ever.

June 5

Matt's going back to California today. He has ROTC Leadership Development Boot Camp coming up, a month in Alabama as an intern, and then another year at Berkeley. I'm so proud of him. Of course, the selfish part of me wants him to stay put right here with us.

I know it's crazy and I'm sure it's a result of having lost my brother in a car accident, but when I have to say 'goodbye' to one of my children, I tend to worry that something terrible might happen to them while they're away from my watchful eye. I don't know why I do this since it just makes me scared. I actually get all panicked and the tears that come to my eyes are not the good, happy, tears – no, these are tears of real grief. I have to stop and remind myself that everyone's perfectly fine! Then I get scared that even thinking about an accident might mean it's going to come true because I've either jinxed fate or had some kind of premonition.

This is an example of how irrational I can be when it comes to my children. I feel so protective of them and yet, I can't protect them at all. They are the three people that really have depended on me and that has given me purpose. I was so proud of my mothering skills. I loved nothing more than cuddling with my little brood, reading them stories at night, tucking them in, kissing them goodnight and watching them sleep. But kids grow up and become independent. They don't need me to take care of them. In fact, sometimes I worry that it's me that has become dependent on them.

Never was this more apparent than the year after my divorce. Matt has always been one of the most reliable, helpful, smartest kids anyone could ever hope to know. He's the consummate Boy Scout, always prepared, always knowledgeable about the "right" thing to do in any situation. When I got divorced, Matt, at age 16, became the man of the house. He helped me with anything that required someone tall, someone strong, or someone who knew how to fix things. Basically, he helped me with everything.

Once, I came running into his room in the middle of the night, telling him the house behind us was on fire and we needed to gather our stuff and get out quickly. Matt ran to my room to look out the window.

"I don't see any fire, Mom."

"It's right there, Matt!" I say, full of adrenaline, rushing around trying to figure out what we should bring and where we should escape.

"Mom, I think it's just a bright light in the neighbor's yard."

I come over to take a look.

"Oh." I let it sink in that our house isn't going to burn down. Then I feel the embarrassment of my false alarm. "It really looked like a fire, with the wind all blowing and everything," I try and convince Matt. He just looks at me skeptically.

"Really, Matt! Come look out the window from the bed. It's like an optical illusion. It really looks like a fire!"

"Everything's gonna be OK, Mom. Do you want to sleep on the floor in my room? Or we can go downstairs and have some hot chocolate?" Matt says with an amused smirk on his face, imitating me and my remedy for anything scary. I actually think hot chocolate sounds pretty good, but I wave him away, close the blinds so I won't see the "fire" and get back into bed. I didn't even ask him to tuck me in.

But things changed during Matt's senior year of high school. It was as if evil aliens invaded his body. He wanted to spend every minute of every day with his girlfriend. The last thing he wanted to do was help his clueless mother! Who would have thought my over-responsible son would turn into a typical, disrespectful teenager? His behavior got so bad that his grandparents threatened to boycott his graduation. Matt overheard me on the phone, defending him, saying how much I loved him, despite his alien-like behavior. When the call was over, he knocked on my bedroom door. I opened it and there he stood, crying, telling me how sorry he was for how he'd been acting. It truly was a Hallmark moment. Aliens gone. I had my son back.

Though it had been a tough year, by the end of it, Matt and I had found a way to reconnect on a deeper level – adult to adult. It was as if we were both coming of age, though he seemed much more prepared than I was to conquer the world. I cried most of the summer in 2005 – the year I drove him out to Berkeley. I was so afraid of being the sole adult in what was left of my little family – just Scotty and me. What if there was some common sense kind of thing that I didn't know about? I heard about some guy who mixed two cleansers together and it created a toxic reaction and he died from the fumes. Poor guy. Just trying to do a little extra cleaning. I remind myself that I rarely do any more cleaning than necessary, so it's unlikely I'll make any mistakes about cleansers.

That was three years ago. We all somehow survived Matt's absence. Matt is more mellow and good-natured than ever. The stresses of that senior year are far behind us. He tells me he loves me often. He hangs out with his little brother. He helps me around the house. He raves about my cooking. And today, I must say goodbye again as he heads back to live his life.

I know I'm much stronger than I was three years ago. I can live without Matt. I'm much more independent and emotionally healthy. This time I won't cry at his departure. I won't even imagine anything about that plane crashing.

June 6

I've invited FB over for dinner to celebrate his birthday. He's only a few months younger than me. I count it as the same age. I know.

90

I wasn't even going to talk to him this year, but we've been chatting over IM a lot and it is a tradition to make dinner together for birthdays. Making dinner is one of my favorite things to do with FB because he's such an awesome cook. We're making a spinach frittata and a salad. All very healthy because he's trying to lose weight. We bring the food out to the patio along with the bottle of wine he's contributed.

We drink enough wine to start talking about our *Match.com* dates. I'm very happy to hear about all of FB's encounters, especially since he seems to be doing quite badly. I don't know if he's leaving out any good dates to spare my feelings, but I'm enjoying the tales of the bad dates.

He went on a picnic with one woman from Boulder who didn't shave her underarms. She started singing as they walked in the park and asked him to join her. Just the thought of this scene makes me burst into giggles. FB has a hard enough time *talking* to someone new so singing is definitely out of the question.

He discussed his 9-11 theories with one of his other dates. He said he sent her an email the next day with some links to sites to support the conspiracy theories. He also asked her if she might want to get together again. He said her reply email simply had three words:"No thank you."

"I told you not to discuss politics until at least the fifth date," I chide him.

"One gal practically kicked me out when I took my shirt off. I am so phat." FB always spells fat like "phat." I don't know if "phat" is maybe the cool way of spelling it or if there is some difference between the two words. I love his big body and I don't think he looks fat at all. He has these wonderful broad shoulders and very muscular arms. I tell him it's hard to believe that anyone would have kicked him out because she thought he had a bad body. "Maybe she just wasn't ready to get physical," I try and reassure him, secretly feeling both alarmed that he had a date that got far enough for him to remove his shirt and relieved that she kicked him out.

"Nope. She just changed her mind when she saw my gut" he argues.

"And what about you?" he asks me. "How have your *Match.com* dates been going?"

I ambiguously tell him that it's going "fine."

91

"And your book? Am I in it?" I bet he thinks it's all about him!

"I haven't decided yet. Probably not." I tell him. "It's my 2008 diary and I've hardly seen you this year. It's about my adventures and my man-of-the-month." I try and make it sound like I've had an exciting date every month. I tell him that last month my May date was the wedding with my handsome friend, Zach. I'm rubbing this in a little, trying to make him sorry that he didn't go to the wedding with me as originally planned. I want him to know that I am getting along just fine without him.

"So, I want to hear more about this problem you're having when you take your shirt off. I think I should take a look at that gut and give you a critique. You know I am a certified phat coach," I tease as I start unbuttoning his shirt. I know it's probably a mistake, but I don't care. He's clearly having no luck with dating and is in need of an ego-boost. And I want to make sure all my parts are still working. I've read those internet chain letters that say that if you don't have sex you get all dried up or something.

Devil: Are we finally going to get some action?

*Angel: Dear, we've been over this. FB is **Former** Boyfriend. You shouldn't even be having dinner with him, let alone a sexual encounter. You deserve someone who loves you.*

Devil: Don't listen to her, Sister! FB stands for Fuck Buddy! Enjoy it!

Angel: Watch your language, Damien!

Devil: Can it, Angelica. I wanna hear this.

At first FB playfully slaps at my hands as I'm fiddling with his buttons, but then he tells me two can play at that game, and he starts taking my shirt off as well. I feel his familiar arms and body. "You appear to have just the right amount of phat," I assure him. "Shall we go upstairs where I can clearly assess the situation?"

We move up to the bedroom. He has his hands around my hips as we go up. It's always that light touch of his that gets to me. My body starts tingling all over in anticipation.

He kisses me in all the right places. He doesn't need to do much. Yes! I can confidently say, my body seems to be in working order! It's been over six months since our last intimate encounter, but it's as though we're able to pick up where we left off. It's not uncomfortable or awkward. Just the opposite. Everything is familiar and easy. We know exactly what the other likes and sex with him, as always, is exciting. I love the feel of his arms around me and want to savor the feeling of his strength and warmth. He kisses me gently and holds me, my back against his front, as we doze. I know he cares about me. There's no way he can fake that tenderness.

"Why did you disappear?" I finally ask him quietly.

He doesn't say anything for a minute and I wonder if he's sleeping – or pretending to sleep.

"You deserve someone better than me," he answers.

Now I'm silent. I know what he means to say is just what the Angel and everyone else tells me: "You deserve someone that loves you." But he doesn't want to talk about love, and neither do I. I just want to lay here and have a night of pretending he loves me.

After awhile I ask him, "Will you be my Mr. June?"

"What does Mr. June have to do? Are you going to take my picture?"

"No, no. It just means I write about you in my book. Are you OK with that?"

"Will you change my name?"

"Sure."

"Can you give me a name like Johnny Cash?"

"No, your name is FB. Do you want me to let you read it first?"

FB thinks for a minute and then he says, "No. Write whatever you want. Don't let me read it until after it's published." I think this is extremely magnanimous of him. FB is really very private and I'm surprised he's given me full permission to write whatever I want. One of our past "issues" has been that I'm quite open and like to talk to my friends about our relationship. He's the opposite. I've gotten very hurt that, for the most part, he keeps our relationship hidden, even from his family and friends.

"Really? Are you sure you're OK with that?"

"Yeah." Then he thinks for a minute. "You're gonna give me some of the profits when it becomes a best seller, aren't you?"

"Sure, I can do that." I roll over and give him a quick kiss and then I go to sleep.

I know FB and I are not really together, but I feel happy. I was so tired of having to constantly remind myself to stay away from him. I am not falling into the trap again of thinking it's anything special. We both are out there in the dating world and that is just fine with me. Especially now that I have reassurance that FB is not enjoying it. I have a little extra boost of confidence just knowing that he still cares about me. I know we we won't get married or anything, but I don't feel so lonely anymore.

Brody and I are out for FAC – Friday Afternoon Club – at Gordon Biersch. Scotty's with Paul, his Dad, on Friday nights and I hate spending nights alone in that big house. Chloe, our Lassie-lookalike Shetland Sheepdog, stays with Scotty, so the house is extra quiet. Even though she can drive me crazy with her hyperness and barks, I miss that disobedient dog. And, of course, I miss Scotty. He's such a good kid. Just having him around – whether he's doing his homework or watching TV or playing the computer – gives me a sense of comfort. When he's gone, the house feels hollow and empty.

Tonight Brody is free for the evening, so we're having dinner and sharing our stories of the week. I casually mention that FB and I got together last week for his birthday. "You slept with him?" Brody is surprised and kind of upset. He seems unusually disturbed by this news. In fact, he actually seems mad. In the four years I've known him, I've never seen him mad. I'm not used to people being mad at me. I'm pretty good about avoiding confrontation. I don't even fight with my ex-husband!

"It's no big deal." I tell him. "Nothing has changed. I just wanted to have sex and so did he. It's been a long time."

"You were doing so well, Vetsky. I thought you weren't ever gonna see that guy again. That you had finally gotten over him."

"I AM over him. It was just sex! You do it all the time! Why are you getting so upset?"

"Because I know guys like him. I AM a guy like him. He DOESN'T LOVE YOU, Vetsky! Can't you get that through your head?"

Now I'M getting mad.

"Don't you think I KNOW he doesn't love me, Brody? Don't you think I tell myself that all the time? I don't need you to remind me. I don't see why you're getting so bent out of shape. You were the one that supplied me with the super-duper-condom when I went out with Marc!"

"This ain't no hump-and-dump, Vetsky. You have feelings for this guy."

"And I suppose you think I should just have sex with people I have no feelings for like YOU do. Well, guess what? That doesn't work for me! You can go around having sex with Ms.-Out-of-Staters and with women who are showing you their man-in-the-boat, and I don't criticize you. I could have lied to you, but I didn't. I had sex with him. So what? I just told you because you're my friend. Now let's drop it."

We talk about other things, but neither one of us has recovered from the unusual outburst. We're both still upset. How dare he judge me for this! He's such a hypocrite. And he is so critical of FB! He doesn't even know him! Just because Brody goes around sleeping with women he doesn't like doesn't mean every other man acts that same idiotic way. FB is *nothing* like Brody. I never should have mentioned this. I hate it that Brody has ruined the little bit of happiness I'd felt about FB. I don't want to go back to feeling sad and rejected. We finish our dinners and say our stilted goodbyes.

June 23

Brody calls me from Chicago. He's out there on business. Or maybe he's hooking up with Ms. Illinois. I don't know. I'm still kind of mad at him. We haven't talked since the "argument." He wants to know why I haven't responded to his email.

"What email?" I ask.

"Don't play innocent, Vetsky. The one with the Trial Agreement"

"I really don't know what you're talking about, Brody."

"Fine. I'll resend it. Check your email."

Date: Mon, Jun 23 at 4:44 PM
From: bro@imdaman.com

Attached below (*once again*) is the "Trial" proposal that I emailed
you days ago   ...... the one that you (Oh internet junkie/SUN
communication expert) are pretending not to have received!

It's the boldest move I have made ...out from under my rock ...   in
years and it gets completely ignored which must mean that you've
chosen Miss- Match.com "so what do you do for a living" coffee's
and dates / and boring ole comfortable ole ...I've got to get laid but
gosh this is really getting old... FB ..and that stands for Fuck Buddy,
.at least in his mind, whether you admit it or not ...instead of a
chance for a real live romantic, caring, funny, handsome, tall   er
than you ,   boyfriend (with a hot tub and a maid) who knows you
better than anyone and STILL *adores* you !!

I suggest we ponder this over some VERY strong Margs at your
favorite (Fish Taco?) restaurant   ...is it possible that we are just a
few shots of tequila away from something really special ???

TRIAL AGREEMENT

The undersigned,   Yvette Francino and T. Brody Anderson
hereinafter referred to in this agreement as "the couple" do hereby
individually and collectively desire to enter into a *"TRIAL"*
(Temporary Romantic Investigational Assimilated Liason) for a period
of 30 days. (hours if YOU are the chicken) During the *"TRIAL"*   the
couple will conduct themselves as "boyfriend and girlfriend" by
keeping each other company, playing tennis, riding bikes, dining out,
traveling to exotic beaches and otherwise having fun together as well
as assisting each other when necessary in DLA (daily living
activities), supporting each other in achieving professional and
personal goals, and last but not least providing each other with an
abundance of, hourly, daily, bi or tri-weekly, (circle one) monogamous
intimate physical expressions of their attraction for one another with
the goal of achieving mutual and simultaneous gratification
whenever possible. The *TRIAL* will not preclude either party from
pursuing platonic friendships and or flirting with the opposite sex. At
the end of the *TRIAL,* both parties agree to return to their previous

level of friendship with no expectations or pressures to continue the *TRIAL*. However, the automatic 30 day expiration will not preclude the parties from entering into another *TRIAL* agreement if   mutually desired.

Signed _____ and _____ date_____

This *is* a bold move for Brody. I can see why he was upset that I didn't respond, but I really hadn't gotten the previous email. Laptop Guy must have thought it was spam and filtered it out. He's protective that way. I don't know how to respond to this. I'm the one that had come up with the whole "Trial Boyfriend/Girlfriend" idea a long time ago in one of our discussions about relationships. I wasn't suggesting the two of us try it – just thinking the concept might help commitmentphobes be a little more open to the idea of getting involved.

I wish I could want this with Brody. I love him as a friend but I don't think of him as a boyfriend. But could I? I respond, telling him he's making progress with his commitmentphobia and that I'll have my lawyers check over the agreement. I warn him that I don't think I'm ready for any contracts, but it would be good to discuss at Wahoos – the fish taco place with the killer margaritas that he refers to in his email – on Friday after work.

June 27 5:30pm

Brody finally shows up, thirty minutes late. He seems a little agitated. Not his usual self. He gets his dinner and I order a second margarita.

"About the contract," I start. "First, my lawyers have told me that since this was my original idea, with patent pending, you should be giving me credit with a trademark symbol somewhere in the agreement."

"Done! Even though I don't believe you have a legal leg to stand on I will gladly give you full credit for the TRIAL idea."

"Secondly," I argue. "I know you well enough to know that as soon as we sleep together you will lose interest in me, so I want the agreement amended to state that I would have access to and will inherit all your money regardless of the outcome of the TRIAL."

97

"No can do, Vetsky. Though during the TRIAL, you're free to spend what you will. Hell, I'll take you on a romantic jaunt to Italy if you want. How's that for a July Adventure?"

"Hmmm. Very tempting offer," I concede.

I get serious. "Brody, I don't want our friendship to change. I like it the way it is. If we change it, it will just get weird, and there's no way we could go back to what we have now. And you know you wouldn't "renew the contract." We both know your pattern. You want what you can't have. I'm the same way."

"I don't get it, Vetsky. I can give you so much more than FB and you choose him over me."

"I'm not choosing him over you!" I'm starting to get mad and emotional again.

"Are you saying you will *never* be anything more than friends with me?" he challenges me.

"I'm saying I don't want to be more than friends with you because I want to make sure we will *always* be friends."

"I have enough friends, Vetsky. If this is never going to change then I'm going to move on. I suggest you do the same with your precious stud-muffin, FB. One of these days you'll realize he is holding you back. He's been holding you back for years and years and years, and you just don't get it."

I think that's a totally unfair statement. I mean how could it be "years and years and years?" That would equate to six years minimum, because "years" is plural, meaning at least two years, repeated three times. I've only been divorced for four and a half years. Brody's logic is totally warped. I don't stop to explain this to him. This has nothing to do with FB and whether or not he's holding me back.

"Are you saying you don't want to be my friend just because I won't have sex with you? All the time we've been friends – it was only because some day you thought you might be able to get me into your bed?" I'm more than mad, now. I'm furious. He's abandoning our friendship over this?

"I don't know, Vetsky. I guess I thought some day it might happen. But now that I know it won't, I don't want to waste any more time."

"You feel like you've been wasting time? I've never kept you from pursuing anyone! How have you been wasting time? Does our friendship mean that little to you?"

"I guess it does." He gets up and leaves Wahoos and drives away.

And so it appears we broke up, even though we were never a couple. I had thought avoiding a romantic relationship offered the benefit of never having a "break up." I had thought he would be my friend forever. But I guess in Brody's mind, we were never really friends.

June 27 7:00pm

A local band plays every Friday night at the Louisville Street Faire during the summer months. Since Friday is my night without Scotty and a lot of my friends show up for the Street Faire, I go almost every week. It's always a fun time with dancing and street vendors. Tonight I'm not feeling in the mood, though. I'm still livid over Brody's abrupt departure. I've never seen him act so rudely. He didn't even say 'Goodbye.' How could he do that to me?

In the old days I would have held one of my pity parties blowing this all out of proportion, crying that I'd lost one of my best friends. But I've read many self-help books and realize that a positive attitude is everything, so I blink back those wimpy tears. He'll be back after the sting of our conversation has worn off. He put himself out there and I said 'no.' He's not used to women saying 'no.' I'm not going to think about this right now. I have this sexy sun dress on and it's a beautiful evening. I'll put this behind me and go have some fun.

"Born in the Flood" is playing tonight. It's a band I don't know, but the place is hopping. I find my group of *Rebuilder* friends standing around a table outside. Zach's there, my attractive Mr. May. I call him "hubby" now, still pretending like I tricked him into marrying me at Megan's wedding. He tells me he's gotten four calls from me in the last week. Apparently, my cell phone has been calling him. I never really figured out how to use my Blackberry, and it must have some kind of weird call-back redial feature. Zach tells me he's been getting calls from me that are just white space or me talking to someone. Oh dear. I don't want Zach to think I'm stalking him. I try to think back if I've had any conversations which would be embarrassing if overheard. I've been bragging about what a good wedding date he was, but he knows all that. I just hope it hasn't called him during any of my recent conversations with Brody! Zach good-naturedly tells me there was nothing incriminating on the phone calls. "Very boring" he tells me. He says he knows I'm just acting like a wife, checking up on him constantly. Mental note: "Remember to put lock on Blackberry or figure out how to disable "stalk" mode."

I wander around, looking at the wares of the street vendors. I enjoy people watching at these Faires. It's a big party with people of all ages, drinking, laughing, and enjoying the summer music. Then I see them. FB is standing at a round table with a bunch of people including a woman who is standing very close to him. I move back, attempting to get in a position behind a crowd where I can see him, but he can't see me.

I sneak back around a bunch of people trying to get a better view. I'm intent on figuring out what's going on with this woman. She's just brought them beers and I can tell from her body language, she's flirting with him. She looks to be about 35, stylish short blond hair, thin, pretty. She's taller than me. (who isn't?) Maybe 5'8"? Could this be a *Match.com* date? They seem to know each other. This isn't a first meeting. They're with a group of about six people, all laughing.

I keep observing intently from my little vantage point. I'm obsessed with watching this scene. FB's back is to me, so I can't see his face, but he seems to be enjoying the attention from this woman. My heart is pounding and the lump is making its appearance again. She kisses him and he's kissing her back. In public! He's never been one to be much into PDA. At least not when he was with me. (I'm talking about Public Displays of Affection, not Personal Digital Assistant.) But there he is, smiling and playfully smooching, right here at the Louisville Street Faire around all these people. He knows I come here every week! Must he flaunt this date right under my nose? The lump is getting bigger, but I will not cry. I am not going to let this get to me. Brody is not right about FB. He may not love me, but I'm more than just a F@#k Buddy (I still can't write the F-word). He's just having a good time and there's certainly nothing wrong with that. So what? So am I.

"What's so interesting?" Zach startles me. He's come up behind me and sees that I'm staring intently at the table with the couple that's making goo-goo eyes at each other. I've just tried to convince Zach that I'm not stalking him and here he is catching me stalking someone else.

"That's FB over there, kissing that woman." I tell Zach. Zach knows all about FB. Well, he doesn't know about the "Mr. June" incident, but he knows he's the guy I'm never supposed to talk about because he's out of my life.

I'm tempted to ask Zach to go with me over to a spot where FB will see us and make out with me. I've already used him at the wedding, though. This "let's make the ex jealous" game is wearing thin, I'm sure. He takes a look and then he gives me a hug as he turns me away from the scene.

"Stop torturing yourself," he says. "Anyway, aren't you supposed to be married to me? Come on, we're all walking over to the Louisville Inn to get some dinner. Come with us."

I tell Zach I've eaten already. I give him a big hug and thank him for being such a good friend and husband.

Then I go home. No one is there, of course. No dog. No kids. No husband. No boyfriend, TRIAL or otherwise, No FB. I have nobody. I make sure my cell phone is turned off so that it doesn't accidentally call anyone. And then I get in my bed and do something I promised myself I wouldn't do. I cry.

Hel-loooo! Have you already forgotten about me? I know we've been working on squelching your illusions that I'm your cyboyfriend, but now I've been cast in the role of 'no one'? Did you forget that I bring you eMale? I'm where your journals are stored? I can even provide you with an alternative FB (FaceBook). Stop the pity party, Princess, and remember, as long as I'm around, you'll never be lonely. You've got more virtual friends than you can count, and your real friends and family are just a high-speed connection away. CellPhone-Guy, is right here in your bedroom, too, ready to play, whenever you are.

July

July Goals
1.   *Adventure: Clear Creek White Water Rafting Trip*
2.   *Love: Shakespeare in the Park with Mr. July*
3.   *Write: Start Blogging Again*

Half the year over. I should be half-way through my goals.

At least I feel OK about my first goal. I'm going White Water Rafting for my July Adventure. It's been two years. The last trip was certainly an adventure – a huge scare, actually. Time for me to face my fears.

I don't feel good at all about the stupid Love Goal. Dating is not sounding appealing at all, but I'm supposed to be writing a book about all this so I can't give up now. My *Match.com* six-month guarantee has come to an end. Since I didn't meet "someone special" I get another six months free. Yippee. (This is a very sarcastic, "Yippee." Note the lack of the typical overused exclamation mark.) I'd be a lot more excited if the guarantee program would just refund my money.

I think I'll ask Michael to be Mr. July and go to Shakespeare in the Park with me. These plays are put on at CU Boulder all summer and I've always wanted to go to one of those performances. Michael used to teach a Shakespeare class at CU so I think he'd be interested. I just hope he doesn't get all weird on me like Brody did. I know it's kind of "cheating" on my Love Goal to go with Michael, but he seemed offended that I didn't ask him to the wedding, and it would be so much easier to go with Michael than with someone new. If I were in better spirits, I'd find a new guy to be Mr. July, but I'm tired and still sad about FB and Brody and in no mood to filter through *Match.com* profiles.

As for the book, well, I'm trying to get more motivated about writing. I've started blogging again – I'm inspired by this guy from Australia, Ian Usher, who has a blog of his own. I'd read about him first a couple of months ago. Zach sent the link out about his Life4Sale story. He put his "life"– his house and all his belongings, time at his job, and time with his friends – up for auction on ebay. A few days ago, I read about him in the news again. The auction got tons of publicity and there were rumors of these outrageous bidding wars. It turns out, these bidders weren't qualified and the final price has ended up less than the value of his house. It's an interesting story, but I'm more intrigued by his next venture: 100 goals in 100 weeks. Ian has this great bucket list of exciting adventures that he's going to achieve in the upcoming two years. He's published his itinerary and has invited others to join him. It would be so cool if I could meet up with him when he's in America and experience one of his goals with him and make that my "adventure" of the month. Unfortunately, he'll be closest to Colorado in mid-October – right when I'll be on vacation in Costa Rica – so I'll probably miss him.

After he does his 100 goals in 100 weeks, he's going to write a book about it. Just like me. Except I'm only doing 12 adventures rather than 100 goals. And my "adventures" are a lot less exciting than his "goals." For example, one of his goals is to climb seven fourteeners in seven days. I'd been *thinking* of climbing *one* fourteener, until I decided that I really didn't want to do that and toured Manitou Springs instead. So, he'll have a lot of material for his book, and I'll basically have just a boring diary, comparable to someone in junior high. He'll probably fall in love, too, while I just wander around searching for dates and going out with friends. Oh! I just had an idea! Maybe, if I have one of my adventures with Ian, he'll fall in love with ME! Then we can both have this great romantic ending for our books! That would work out perfectly for my "Fall in Love" goal. And I'd capitalize on Ian's fame. All of Ian's fans would be interested in reading my book as a kind of "parallel story" to his.

I email him. Even though he must get tons of email, he responds almost immediately! I google him, too, and he's pretty cute! (Note that I'm back to overusing exclamation marks. My mood is improving!) I tell him I'm doing an adventure a month, and, if possible, I'd like to join him for one of his goals when he's in America. I resist telling him that we are going to fall in love, though. I don't want to ruin the ending of his book for him.

I'm glad to have a plan to fall in love with Ian Usher. It makes it a little less painful to think about FB with that woman I saw him kissing at the Street Faire.

fb>hey!
yf>hey.
Should I mention I saw him being all kissy face with that woman? I'll just come off as jealous. Be cool.
fb>what's up?
yf>not much... I meant to tell you, I saw you the other night at the street faire.
So much for being cool.
fb> you were there? I didn't see you.
yf>yeah...you seemed occupied.
fb>I was there with some old work friends.
yf>looked like a pretty good "friend"
fb>lol. yeah, I guess she was into me.
Ya think?
yf>looked like you were into her, too.
fb>lots of issues
yf>like?
fb>she voted for Bush, for one.
Ahh. I feel much better now. I know the relationship will never last.
yf>you looked happy.
fb>no TBN
TBN - "The Big Nasty" is FB's code word for "sex." I'm sure he doesn't think of sex as "nasty" but FB heard sex referred to as "The Big Nasty" in a movie once and so TBN has became his "sex" word. Kind of like "phat" is his word for "fat." I'm not sure why he's telling me that he and kissy-face-lady didn't have TBN, but I'm feeling infinitely better. Despite all our ups and downs, I don't think he's ever slept with anyone else.
yf>Are you going out with her?
fb>I suppose.
yf>stay away from Bush and you'll be good
*Bush was **my** code word for "sex". Since FB hates Bush (the President) I've often used the "Bush" word teasingly with FB, thinking I was being very clever when I said something like "stay away from Bush." However, I just recently learned that "Bush" is slang for "pubic hair" not "sex." Figures that I'd even get my sex slang words wrong.*
fb>lol

Michael and I are having our traditional Starbucks coffee and danishes. My insomnia is so bad that I feel like a zombie. Normally, I'd be bragging about how I'm following through on my action plan to find love and encouraging him to do the same, but not this week.

"If you've met someone, please don't tell me about it, OK?"

"I got nothing to tell." This is Michael's standard response when I ask him the usual, "Did you meet anyone this week?"

"Good. Because I'm in danger of going into a deep depression and I need your full attention this month. I may even need you to be Mr. July."

I tell Michael all about Brody and FB and how sad I was last weekend.

"I really wanted to be the one to find someone else first. I'm better now, though, because I'm sure this thing with the kissy-face-lady won't last."

"How do you know?"

I tell Michael about the IM conversation.

"He'd never seriously date a Republican." I tell him. "But he did look very happy at the Street Faire. I don't know if it was "drunk happy" or "love happy." I just know he doesn't look that way when he's around me. I really need to move on. Brody's right about that."

Michael listens to my drama and doesn't judge me at all or tell me I was stupid for sleeping with FB. He seems to understand completely. I complain that Brody wasn't understanding at all.

"He just walked out on me at Wahoos! He as good as said that our friendship meant nothing to him! I'm running out of Flirt Buddies. Chet has a girlfriend, FB is out again, and Brody has decided he doesn't even want to be my friend. I need you to pick up the slack!"

"Gee, I feel so flattered."

"I'm sorry. But I'm tired and I need a Mr. July to go with me to Shakespeare in the Park this month. Will you go?"

"I go every year. Shakespeare's my thing, ya know."

"Yes, I know. So you'll be an ideal Mr. July! My first pick for sure! Much better than Chet or Brody or FB."

"What about Zach? Am I better than Zach?"

Michael's still brooding that I invited Zach to the wedding, claiming he was my "most handsome" friend.

"Oh yes. Zach probably doesn't know anything about Shakespeare."

"OK, then. I suppose I can be Mr. July. But you'd better give me a good write-up in your book."

"The best."

July 6

I get an email from my friend, Sarah with details of the raft trip.

Date: Sun, Jul 6 at 6:27 AM
From: PWPSarah@msn.com
Subject: Rafting is planned for July 12th!!
Hi Yvette—

It was good to hear from you! Below is the e-mail that went out to everyone that said they might be interested in going. I think we will have somewhere between 10-15 of us based on the last reservation count and what everyone has said.

Looking forward to seeing you!! It's been a while!

Sarah

If you would like to join us for a day of rafting on Saturday, July 12th:

We are planning to do the 'Ultimo':

$87 Adults

This is the most consistent whitewater available on the Front Range, and almost the state. If action is what you are after then this is for you. We start off at our office on the banks of Clear Creek above the town of Lawson. Begin your day reveling in all the excitement of the Kamikaze, and then enjoy a tasty lunch prepared on the spot by your guides. Continuing downstream, please digest your lunch before plunging into the awesome class

IV rapids of the Lower Canyon, including Ejector, Double Knife, Deep Hell, and Terminator, just to name a few. An adventure for the brave of heart! Be prepared for a workout.

Minimum age 15
Clear Creek location

I met Sarah a few years ago when I was active in Parents Without Partners (PWP). She's a sweetie. She and her boyfriend, Tom, had served on the Board for several years. I haven't been a member for the past couple of years – Scotty never really got into it and most of the events were too far. The group became less active recently with the advent of meetup.com and meetin.org. But I think a lot of the people on Sarah's email list are former PWPers. It will be good to see some old friends and maybe some new faces!

I'm nervous about doing the Advanced Trip. That's the same trip I was on when we had the accident two years ago. Even the names of the rapids: Ejector, Double Knife, Deep Hell, and Terminator, conjure up difficult memories and make my heart beat a little faster. But it wouldn't be much of an Adventure if I was doing a wimpy, beginner trip.

July 12

It looks like all the former Parents Without Partners are now Parents With Partners. Six couples, three teen-agers (including a hot girl in a bikini) and me. I am so tired of couples and hot young girls. Not that I'm really jealous of a teenage girl. It's just that next to her, I feel like a frumpy old lady. I try to be happy for these people, but I keep wondering why it is that everyone seems to be able to find a partner but me!

As I'd suspected, most of this crowd are people that I met when I was in PWP. Elizabeth and Kurt are a very "progressive" couple. Elizabeth, a friendly woman from Australia, amuses me with her sexual openness. She's always encouraged me to be more experimental – maybe try a "threesome?" I told her I was still working on a "twosome," but once I had that mastered, maybe I'd try for the more advanced "threesome."

Devil: I think I'd be having a lot more fun if I were Elizabeth's inner-Devil.

Angel: Dear, don't listen to him. You're providing the Devil with plenty of challenge.

I tell the group about my book and that I'd been hoping there would be some single guy whose lap I'd fall into when the raft was bouncing around, but that it looks like there's no one available. Kurt reassures me that he's available for any lap catching. As I said, he and Elizabeth have this very "open" relationship. Then, perhaps to prove he has no problem with touch, he puts his hands under my shirt, rubbing my chest area above my tummy and below my breasts. Kurt and Elizabeth may be fine with this community touchy-feely stuff, but I'm feeling just a tad uncomfortable. You could say, I'm *feeling out of place*, but I think it was Kurt that was guilty of that, if you know what I mean. (I love these cheesy puns.) I regret mentioning the whole topic of my singleness. Now it's getting way too much attention.

Elizabeth tells me that she has a friend, Amy, and Amy has a friend who she's trying to set up. This is a very indirect set up...a friend of a friend that has a friend. I would have preferred the setup to be a friend of a friend rather than adding an extra degree of separation there, but, hey, I can be flexible. I say 'sure' and before I know it Elizabeth is on the cell phone calling Amy. She hands the cell phone over to me and Amy starts telling me about this guy that she wants to set up. "He's 41 years old, cute, married for two years, scuba diver,..." Back up. *Married*? Did she say *married*?

I interrupt her. "Did you mean he's been divorced for two years?"

"No, he's married."

"Um. I'm looking for a single guy."

Elizabeth motions for me to give her the phone back. "She's *vanilla*, Amy. Didn't you say there was a *vanilla* guy you knew?"

"OK, she's got the right guy now." Elizabeth hands me back the phone.

"So sorry," Amy apologizes, saying she was confused. OK new guy. "Blond, two kids, mountain climber, very active, in his forties. What can you tell me about yourself?"

I'm tempted to tell Amy I'd classify myself more as *French Vanilla*. Or how about *Pistachio*? That sounds sexy in a nutty kind of way. Vanilla sounds so *boring*. Should I brag about how often I turn on my laptop?

Devil: You are soooooooo vanilla. You're more vanilla than vanilla. You're like vanilla lite.
Angel: There's no shame in vanilla, Dear. It's pure and sweet and has a soothing, mild flavor.

I tell Amy my *Match.com* screen name and tell her she can let her friend read my profile and contact me if he's interested. It's a rather hasty goodbye as we're being called to gear up. Since this friend of a friend of a friend hangs around with non-vanilla-types, I'm guessing he'll want more flavor than I have to offer. Honestly, even though it would make a good chapter for my book, I've already got Michael lined up for Mr. July, so I'm not really in a rush to be set up with anyone, regardless of their flavor.

We don our wet suits and helmets. I rent booties, too, remembering how freezing my feet were last time I went rafting. The river water is provided by the melting snow of the mountains and it's icy cold.

Here comes the safety speech. You know how when you're on an airplane they give you all that canned hoo-ha about oxygen masks, nearest exists, and buckling up? You know how you usually just ignore it because you've heard it a million times? I mean, is there anyone out there that really doesn't know how to operate a seatbelt? Now, if I'd been witness to one of my friends having a near-death experience, trapped in a seatbelt, and unable to release herself because she hadn't listened to the unbuckling instructions, I would pay a little more attention next time I heard that speech. (I also would have serious concerns about my friend's lack of practical knowledge of common household items, yet feel a bit of a bond with her.) The point is, once you've been a firsthand witness to an accident, you listen more carefully to safety precautions.

For this reason, I listen intently when they go over the safety rules.

"Hold on to the T-bar on the top of the oar at all times. Most rafting accidents occur by letting go of that T-bar."

Yup. That happened during the first half of the raft trip, that day in June, 2006. Lindee was the first casualty, getting smacked in the face with the T-bar of an oar, breaking her nose during a rapid. The raft hadn't flipped, but Eileen had fallen into the river. She was white with cold and fright, but quickly able to get back into the raft. When we made it to the appointed lunch stop, bloody-faced Lindee was bussed off to the hospital. Eileen, wrapped in blankets, was still shivering, but determined to meet her fears head-on and tackle the second half of the trip.

We were a group of 12 – well, now 11 with Lindee gone – split between two rafts. We were all *Rebuilder* graduates – still "rebuilding" our lives post-divorce. I guess one of the things we *Rebuilders* like to do is go out and live life! Have Adventures! Prove we're brave and will survive, with or without a mate. Gloria Gaynor's, *I Will Survive*, is our theme song. And so, despite Eileen's very shaken state – both physically and emotionally – she'd decided to continue.

Honestly, I'm surprised the rafting company let a group of whitewater-novices get out on the river that day. The water was high and fast – they told us it was about as fast as they'd ever seen it. It was thrilling, no doubt – more thrilling than any roller coaster I've ever been on. But we were inexperienced. They told us during the safety speech to expect the rafts to overturn. They guaranteed that "someone would be swimming" before the end of the day. We all smiled at each other nervously as we signed the release forms – this was going to be fun!

Despite the morning accident, we all decided to go on. We'd come this far and, those of us that hadn't gotten hurt were having a blast. We patted ourselves on the back. We're GREAT rafters!

The second half of the day was harder and faster. One rapid after another. We all were constantly drenched by high, frigid, splashes as we worked our oars hard to the guide's call. Even the guide seemed nervous, barking the commands at us, and reprimanding us for not staying in sync, warning us we would flip if we didn't pay attention. We laughed with relief and high-fived with our oars with each success, but we didn't have long between rapids to celebrate. Some of the rapids were incredibly steep. I felt daring and strong, as our raft angled precariously over rocks and waterfalls. It was exhilarating and petrifying. We let out whoops and screams as we rushed down the river, full speed. We saw other rafts overturning, but somehow ours made it down with no problems. "We survived!" we laughed, relieved when we got to the bottom. "That was AWESOME!" We were jazzed. Our guide brought us to a cove, where we waited for the other rafts to get through those Indiana Jones-like final rapids watching for the second half of our group – our friends in another raft.

We watched the other rafts come down. Some, like ours, made it without capsizing, others flipped and recovered, others temporarily lost a passenger or two to the river who then got pulled back in. One by one, the rafts made it down, but there still was no sign of the raft with our friends. Then we saw an empty raft coming down. We nervously looked around in the water wondering if our friends had been rescued or whether they were still out swimming the rapids. And then we saw it.

An empty kayak rushing through the river, dragging a body face down. Our guide, along with a couple of other guides swim out to the kayak. They turned the body face up, revealing Eileen's blue face and lifeless body.

We were shooed up and away from the scene, as a crew worked at resuscitating Eileen. Ambulances and rescue workers gathered. We got word that she was dead. The others from the raft had eventually made their way out of the water and were trudging, dirty, injured, and in shock, trying to find the group.

As we huddled around, crying at the tragedy, we saw a crew bring up Eileen's body and put her in an ambulance. They'd been able to revive her, we were told, but she wasn't out of the woods yet. Two of the others also needed emergency care and were rushed off to the hospital. Allyson had deeply gashed her leg on a rock and Randall was suffering from shock and hypothermia. It was a long night, and we all did survive, but it gave me a new respect for the power of the river, and for listening to safety instructions.

Today I'm going down the same river. Stupid or brave? It's a question I've been asking myself a lot when I think about the definition of "adventure." I survived the first time. Why am I purposely putting myself at risk a second time? The water is fast, but nothing like that day two years ago. We have fun. We laugh. Kurt tries to touch my boobs. There are no accidents. Life is good. I come to the conclusion that every day is an adventure. Every day is a risk. We can be scared or we can be confident and have fun. Who wants to stay cooped up in a safe little haven instead of living? I may be vanilla, but I'd like to think there's a little bit of hot fudge in me, too.

"What should our song be?"

"Our song?"

"Yes. I have special songs with lots of friends. Songs that remind me of those people and then when that song comes on the radio, I think of that person and it's like I'm sharing a special memory. Like Brody, for example. Our song is *Here Without You* by 3 Doors Down because that was his ring tone and I really like that song, so it became our song. Now whenever I hear that song, I think of him."

Michael still doesn't seem convinced that we need a song. Maybe I'm pushing my luck here. He's doing the Mr. July thing, but it seems that suggesting a special song is overstepping some boundary. Michael has also just finished telling me stories about two different women friends who have the hots for him. He has told me how this makes him very uncomfortable and now he's avoiding these women.

"I don't understand why it's necessary to avoid someone who has the hots for you. It's flattering! Enjoy the attention!"

"These women are certifiably insane."

I'm not convinced that the women in question are insane. Maybe Michael just thinks they're insane because he feels weird about being around someone who has the hots for him when he doesn't have the hots for them.

"Well they *must* be insane if they're interested in you." I tease him. "If you thought I was interested in more than friendship, would you call me insane and start avoiding me?"

Michael gives me a questioning look.

"I'm not saying I *am* interested in more than friendship," I quickly add. "I'm just asking if you thought I was, would you avoid me? Because part of the deal with the man of the month is that it has to be a date, ya know. None of this wingman stuff. I don't care if the hottest chick ever is there, your job as Mr. July is to be paying attention to ME."

After the Mr. January date with Boy-Toy Buddy, Chet, I feel compelled to drive this point home.

"Yeah, yeah. I know it's a date," Michael assures me.

"Then how come you're acting all weird about a song?"

113

"Usually going on a date doesn't involve having a song."

"Well, I like having a song. And I want to be free to have a romantic July date without you going all weird on me and thinking I'm some lunatic that wants to jump your bones."

"What do you mean by *romantic* date? Is there to be swimming in each others eyes from across the table?"

"Shakespeare in the Park is romantic. Love's Labour's Lost is romantic. It's a romantic date."

I don't really know if Love's Labour's Lost is romantic since I haven't studied the Cliff Notes as I've been meaning to do. But it has the word Love in it and it's Shakespeare, so it must be romantic.

July 19

I've decided on a good song for Michael and me. Last year, when we were driving home from getting the Christmas Tree, Chasing Cars came on the radio and we sang it out loud.

Date: Sat, Jul 19 at 12:31 PM
From: yvette.francino@gmail.com
Subject: Our song

Our song is Chasing Cars by Snow Patrol. And even though it might be considered a "love song" which may make you squirm with discomfort, I think the lyrics could be interpreted as friends who talk about love, trying to understand it.

> *I don't know where, confused about how as well*
> *just know that these things will never change for us at all.*

These lines seem to make sense for our relationship. As we talk about all our ups and downs with love, we don't know where or how we'll find it, but that our friendship won't change. (At least that's how I'm choosing to interpret these lines.)

> *Let's waste time, chasing cars, around our heads.*
> *I need your grace to remind me, to find my own.*

These lines remind me of our mornings at Starbucks, sometimes rehashing the same discussions trying to make sense of our

114

feelings. Hearing the other's perspectives helps us to better understand how we really feel.

And, of course, this is also "our song" because I remember when it came on the radio and we were singing it on our way back from getting the Christmas Tree.

So... in short... it's perfect for "our song". I'll think of you whenever I hear it (which is often, since it's one of my favorite songs!)

Y (your new girlfriend now that we have a "song". ;-))

July 23

Michael picks me up at 5:30. He's wearing a white polo shirt and khakis. He's looking cool with his shades, ready for our "romantic date." He opens the door for me and helps me up into his Expedition, following proper "date" etiquette.

We get to campus and Michael guides me to the big, beautiful park on campus between all the main buildings that is referred to as the 'quad.' This is his old stomping grounds. He reminisces about the days he was studying and teaching at CU, showing me the various buildings, and telling me the stories of the time when he was actually living in his office, sleeping on a couch while he was going through his divorce. We all have stories – memories – that we want to share. Being here brings back a lot of memories for Michael and he seems to be feeling nostalgic. Finishing his PhD was something on his life's To Do List. Being here again reminds him of that unfulfilled dream. But it also reminds him of his teaching days and he seems content and at home.

We get to a nice picnic spot on the big grassy area and Michael lays out a blanket. He opens the basket he's brought filled with French bread, brie, grapes, and wine. He's doing very well with the romance.

"I'm impressed!"

"I can be romantic." I can see Michael feels proud that he is playing the Mr. July role so well. We get settled on the blanket. The summer early evening air is beautiful. Just the right temperature with the sun lowering. It smells like summer in the park. Scents of flowers and trees.

Michael has packed everything in that little basket. He even has wine glasses which he fills and we toast to our date. I pull out the notes I've printed from the Internet about Love's Labour's Lost and ask Michael to explain certain quotes. Michael, the expert, falls into teacher mode and enlightens me on the nuances of the relationships of the characters and some of the background on the play. His thesis was something to do with Shakespeare, so he really is the Shakespearean guru. Michael and I have a common interest in words and writing. He, of course, is much more literary than I am. What I write could hardly be considered *literature*. Blogs and journals – those are not the works of a "real" writer. But Michael respects my interest in writing, whatever that writing is, and he's very supportive in my quest to write a book. If he thinks it's a pipe dream, he keeps that to himself.

We lounge on the blanket and talk about Shakespeare, words, poetry and writing. I could talk to Michael for hours and never run out of things to say. Our conversations often go off on tangents and we have to tell each other to "hold that thought" so we can finish one conversation before we get to a whole new topic. But tonight, I'm not as talkative. I'm enjoying just being here. The atmosphere has the exact element of romance that I'd hoped for. I lay on the blanket and take deep breaths of the summer air, savoring it.

Michael's still chatting.

"Shhh. I'm listening to our song."

He looks at me like I'm crazy. There's no music.

"It's playing in my head." Even though I don't want to ruin the moment with my singing I remind him of the lyrics.

If I lay here, if I just lay here
Would you lie with me, and just forget the world.

Calls for seating interrupt my reverie, and we move over to the outdoor amphitheater to watch the play. Michael gets us more wine and we watch as the actors recite the lines that we'd just been discussing. It's one of those nights that is gorgeous in every way. I'm tempted to link arms with Michael, hold his hand, and lay my head on his shoulder. This is probably because the wine has made me very sleepy and cuddly and very fond of Michael. But I know he'd start to get nervous, just like he did when I suggested the song. He's being such a great Mr. July, and I don't want to ruin it by making him uncomfortable.

The play ends. We pack up and head back to the car and Michael drives me home. He walks me up to my door and I know we're both wondering whether or not this date is going to end in a kiss. It's awkward. That in itself is weird. Michael is one person I feel like I can tell anything. We've discussed everything, including kissing. Michael's a good kisser and he knows it. Our first kiss was in a coat closet at his holiday ball two and half years ago. But he and I have both talked so often about other relationships – and I know, too well, how he withdraws at the hint that a woman wants more than he wants to give. Come to think of it, I do that, too. Maybe we will both be trapped forever still hoping to find that feeling we had with our former loves – that infatuated feeling of desire that neither of us seem to be able to find for anyone else.

Michael's a lot taller than me, so whenever I give him a hug goodbye at Starbucks, I stand on a step. Tonight I stand on the upper doorstep in our traditional hug-goodbye pose. He's still hesitating. I know he wants to please me and do the right thing – to be the perfect Mr. July – but not mislead me. I settle the unspoken question by giving him a big hug. "Thou art a noble friend for whomst I will show my love with a deep embrace. For is it not more fitting that hearts should lock than lips?" He smiles at my fake Shakespeare and spouts off a real quote, which I can't repeat now because I don't remember it, but it sounds good. I'm sure it meant, "I love you, too, you nut." And Mr. July exits the scene, humming the tune of "Chasing Cars" as he waves goodnight.

I don't know where, confused about how as well
Just know that these things will never change for us at all.

To be, or not to be, that is the question:
Whether 'tis nobler to simply spin my lowly drive
To the pings and fondling of lonely fingers,
Or to protect myself against a surge of troubles
To sleep, perchance to dream—ay, there's the rub:
For in that sleep mode what dreams may come,
When I have shut down off *this Ether net,*
Must give us pause—the key pressed by Yvette

~ Laptop Guy (aka RAMlet)

August

August Goals
1.   *Adventure: Long's Peak*
2.   *Love: Go out with a new guy – and keep going out – at least 5 dates*
3.   *Write: Writer's Group*

I hear there are a group of *Rebuilders* that are going to climb Long's Peak this month. I've got a good set of lungs, so I think I'll join them for my August Adventure. When I say I have a good set of lungs, I'm really talking about lungs. (In my youth, I sort of remember boys using that phrase to indicate that girls had big breasts.) I know talking about lungs isn't as sexy as talking about breasts, but the fact remains, when climbing a 14'er (mountain peaks that are 14,000 feet or higher) where the air is thin, good lungs are more important than big breasts.

I've been taking it easy lately with the love goal, but now it's time to get out of my comfort zone and meet someone new. This time I'm not going to be the one to back away. I am going to keep seeing Mr. August, whomever he ends up being, for at least five dates. No matter what kind of weird habits or idiosyncrasies he might have, I am going to look beyond those and find all there is to love about this new man. If he doesn't like me, I won't give up, knowing that eventually he'll see my inner beauty and be smitten.

As for writing, I joined a Writer's Group last month and I love it! Lori, the facilitator, gives these University-level-like-lectures about various topics. Then we critique different essays or stories that people in the group have submitted. I'm probably the only person in the group that's a total novice. I'm feeling out of my league. I've never published *anything* but a blog. But I've been claiming all year that I'm going to write a book, so I guess I'd better figure out exactly how that's done. Lori offered to give me an hour's worth of coaching on my writing if I'd babysit her seven-year-old son. Sounds like a good deal to me.

I'm at the movies with a friend, Janet. Janet and I don't know each other well. We both have a mutual friend, Lauren. Or I should say we *had* a mutual friend, Lauren. Janet and Lauren are no longer friends. Lauren has been dating Bill for the past year and a half, and hence, we rarely see her anymore. This is the reason that Janet and Lauren "broke up." I know this term is usually used to describe the dissolution of a romantic partnership, but I've learned that it can apply to the dissolution of a friendship as well. Personally, I understand and don't hold it against my friends when they find a romantic partner that bumps me off their priority list. That's how it goes and I totally get it. Once you get into a primary relationship, you have to invest in it, and there really isn't much time to be running around with your single friends. So, that's why Janet and I are at this movie. We single people have to stick together.

We've just gotten out of the matinée viewing of *Sex and the City* at the AMC Theater at Flatirons Mall about a mile from my home. There's a relatively cute guy who is handing out fliers in the theater. He looks too young for me, but I do have my goal to consider. He hands me one of the fliers and starts explaining it to me – it's a free ticket to the showing of a movie next Wednesday night. It looks like a shoot-em-up-adventure type, so I'm not really interested in the movie, but I'm always excited about getting a freebie. They're just trying to get a target audience reaction, so all we have to do is fill out a survey after we watch the movie.

When Janet gets out of the bathroom, I tell her about the deal. I bring her over to the flier guy and she asks for one of the free tickets. He's kind of hesitant, not handing over the flier, saying it's not for everyone. Janet and I are confused. He hems and haws.

"This is the hardest part of my job," he says. "We're targeting a specific age range so I'm going to have to ask to see your ID," he says to Janet. On closer examination of the flyer, it says that it is for people between the ages of 30 and 54. Janet is 51. She is indignant. She shows her ID, gets the ticket, but questions the guy about why they are limiting it. "I know, it's stupid," he says. "Sorry."

Janet and I head over to Gordon Biersch which is right next to the theater and sit on the outside patio with margaritas to discuss the movie.

I try to make conversation, hoping to distract Janet from worrying about the faux pas. "Wasn't that a ridiculous looking bird-hat Sarah Jessica Parker was wearing for her wedding? That's supposed to be fashionable?" Janet nods her head in agreement, but doesn't further expand on the hideous hat. I switch tracks.

"I liked the movie, but it was kind of a cliché ending, don't you think?" One thing I'd always liked about the HBO series was that (even though all that rich New York fashion stuff was totally unrealistic) up until the last episode, at least the relationships seemed *real*. I could relate to the whole "he's just not that into you" relationship between Big and Carrie. But then on the last episode and certainly in the movie, Mr. Big ends up being the hero, in love with Carrie at last – a perfect little fairy tale, happily ever after ending. The plot of many a romantic comedy is the same:

1.   Girl loves Boy.
2.   Boy doesn't want to commit.
3.   Girl is sad but "moves on".
4.   Boy realizes he is in love with Girl.
5.   Boy and Girl get married.

Jerry McGuire, Something's Gotta Give, When Harry Met Sally, and just about every other romantic movie all follow that basic story line. And now *Sex and the City* can be added to the list, which is really ironic, because I hear the book, *He's Just Not That Into You,* was inspired from an episode of *Sex and the City* (the HBO series). As the book points out, women have a hard time letting go and moving on. Well, maybe that's because we watch all these chick flicks where the Boy eventually figures out he loves the Girl. If we keep seeing that story, obviously we're going to think that's the way it works. But it doesn't work that way in real life. Readers, beware! *My* book is real life. In real life, stuff like Boy meets Kissy Face Republican (undoubtedly getting to the TBN stage of the relationship by now) and Girl is Lonely and Sad happens. I don't get to have a convenient little ending in which FB finally figures out he loves me. I really thought he would have broken up with The Republican by now, but it doesn't seem to be happening.

Janet's not listening to me. She doesn't care about *Sex and the City* or FB and his Republican girlfriend. She's still upset that the flier guy asked for her ID, but he hadn't asked for mine. She's saying 51 is the worst age. Way worse than 50. I don't bring it up, but I'm pretty sure 52 is going to be even worse. And then, tragedy will strike at 55, because we won't even be eligible for those free tickets to adventure movies.

Flier Guy sees us sitting at Gordon Biersch and comes over to our table. He steps over the iron gate separating the GB patio from those people wandering the mall, and sits at our table with us.

"Do you ladies like karaoke?" I think he's trying to make up for his earlier foot-in-mouth-moment, but it's not working.

Janet gives him the evil eye. "Do you have to be under 50 to go?" she asks dryly.

It's clear flier-guy likes me best (with Janet giving him hate looks, that's not surprising) and I'm tempted for a minute to take him up on the offer. I do have this pressure to find Mr. August. Janet has already declined the offer, and I feel relatively confident that if I deserted her in favor of flier-guy she might go out and get voodoo dolls representing both me and flier-guy. Besides, I'm pretty sure flier-guy is the type of karaoke-singing-attention-hog who wants to sing every song. The type you just want to tell to sit down and let someone else have a chance. I think this because I mentioned I hate it when people do that at karaoke, and he got all defensive. So he went off to karaoke without us.

Listening to Janet talk about all the injustices of aging and being single, I realize that that's what I must sound like. It's kind of unattractive. Not Janet. The negativity. Janet's attitude is totally understandable. If some dork had assumed I was older than 54 I'd be in a bad mood about it, too. But this is a good eye-opener for me. Suddenly 48 is sounding much better. I vow to not complain about being an older single anymore.

August 7

Lori has reviewed some of my writing. When I ask her if she thinks I could ever really write a book, she's encouraging, yet not promising.

"It could take years. But you have to believe in yourself." she advises. I'm not really sure I want to take years. I'm having enough trouble staying motivated to write at all. I tell Lori that the more I hang around serious writers, the more I realize how little talent I have. Lori says that's a good sign. It means I'm recognizing the difference between good and bad writing. "There are four stages of competence." she tells me. "Unconscious Incompetent, Conscious Incompetent,

Conscious Competent, and Unconscious Competent." Apparently, now that I realize I'm a bad writer, I'm a Conscious Incompetent, which is a step above Unconscious Incompetent when I sucked and just didn't know it. Lori assures me this is a normal phase for a writer, and it's a good thing. Now that I know about my incompetence, I can work towards Conscious Competence. And some day, when I can write well without even trying, I'll become an Unconscious Competent.

I can see why Lori's a good writer's coach. I'm feeling motivated and excited about having moved to the state of many writer wannabes: Conscious Incompetent.

August 9

Girl's night out! A bunch of women from the Spring *Rebuilders* Class are meeting for drinks and dancing downtown. I'm flattered that they invited me. They were all participants in the class, in the midst of divorce, and I was a volunteer – supposedly past all those painful emotions. I'm not quite the partier that these ladies are. But tonight it's time to cut loose. Maybe it will be the night I meet my Mr. August.

August 9 11:00pm

Woo Hoo! I'm dancing with this really cute guy. His name is Lucas and he's got this fantastic Austrian accent. About 5'10". Dark blond hair and glasses. Very cute. He's a neurosurgeon here on business. The neurosurgeon part is good. (I'm kind of into brainiacs.) The here on business part is bad. How am I going to be able to get my requisite five dates in if he's only here for a few more days?

Hold on. We're smoochin' now. That's right... I'm smoochin' on the dance floor right in front of everyone just like a modern day woman. OK, maybe I'm acting more like a drunk teenager than a modern day woman, but I don't care. I'm footloose and fancy free!

Devil: You oughta drink tequila shots more often.
Angel: I hope he doesn't have any communicable diseases.

Lucas and I exchange numbers. He's staying at The Renaissance Hotel in Louisville, about ten minutes from where I live. I'm definitely counting tonight as Date #1. We're going out to dinner tomorrow night, so that will be Date #2. I may have to just kind of squeeze Dates #3-5 in tomorrow somehow, too. Maybe we can go to

123

four different places (the last being his hotel?) and that will count as five dates. Yay! Mr. August, I've found you! Now, where are those luscious lips?

I meet Lucas at his hotel. He still looks as good in the sober light of day as I'd vaguely remembered him. I wasn't sure if the chemistry was simply due to our drunken state last night. But no. I'm completely hung-over and he still looks really cute.

We drive together over to The Huckleberry in Louisville. The big purple building on Main Street is one of my favorite places to eat. When Lucas asked me for a suggestion of where we could have dinner, this is the first Louisville location that came to mind. I later realize that this would have been a better choice for breakfast or lunch if I'm trying to portray myself as "cool" 'cause it's not exactly chic. It's kind of got this cozy bed and breakfast feel to it, but the menu choices are things like meatloaf or chicken. This isn't first date kind of dining. It seems more like old married couple dining. But Lucas still seems very interested in me despite my homebody dining choice.

We look over the menu, smiling up at each other.

"So, have you ever been married?" I ask. Perhaps it's too soon to ask this question. It is kind of personal. But, I'm certainly not equipped to discuss neurosurgery and I'm not ready for him to learn how ignorant I am about world events.

"Yes."

"So you're divorced?"

"No." He says this with a little rise to his voice at the end, sort of as though we're playing the 20-questions game and I'm getting closer.

"Widower?"

"No." Again, getting closer.

I can't figure out the answer to this puzzle. "Separated?"

"No." He decides to give me the answer to this riddle. "I'm married."

"Married?" Oh my God! I was kissing a married man last night! And now I'm on a date with a married man! I immediately become paranoid. Will his wife find out and hunt me down? I momentarily wonder if this would bump my status out of the *vanilla* category that I was cast in by my alternative-lifestyle friend, Elizabeth. Not that I'm proud or happy that Mr. August is married, but at least it's not boring.

I immediately change from flirt mode to friend mode.

"Do you have any children?"

"Yes, a daughter" he says proudly and brings up a photo of a cute little blond four-year-old on his iPhone. It's very odd that this is all disclosed as though there's nothing unusual about the situation. No explanation or apology. He's just a married guy out here in the US, kissing women (or at least me – not sure if there are others, but that wouldn't be too surprising) going out on dinner dates.

"I'm not sure if this is a cultural thing, but American married men usually don't kiss women, other than their wives." I don't mention the non-vanilla Kurt or his flavorful friends.

"When they are 4000 miles away from home, they do. We are all the same."

I think this is a rather presumptuous statement and insulting to the male population. Certainly there are some men out there that are faithful to their wives. I suggest that maybe Lucas should be paying attention to his wife and little girl right now. Not to me.

"They're sleeping now." He really doesn't see anything wrong with this situation. He's suggesting that we go back to his hotel room after dinner.

Devil: Go for it! You wouldn't be cheating on anyone. If he wants to screw up his marriage, that's his problem. He's a big boy and can figure out what he wants.

Angel: Heavens no, Dear! Think of his wife! Think of his child!

Devil: Are you going to be boring old vanilla for the rest of your life?

"I really can't," I tell him. The fact that he'd cheat has made me lose all interest in him. Even if he were single – he's from Austria!

"If I hadn't told you I was married, would you have joined me at the hotel then?"

"Yes." I say this confidently now that I know it's not going to happen. I hate that damn devil always telling me that I'm too boring or scared. Of course, I draw the line on messing around with married men.

"Then I made a mistake in telling you."

"No, I'm glad you were honest with me." It's a little ironic that I'm commending him for his honesty.

"Don't you worry about cheating? Will it be worth a divorce it if your wife finds out?"

"My wife would not divorce me over this."

"It's accepted? Then it *is* a cultural thing. 'Cause I can tell you, here in the US, most of us really don't like it when our spouses cheat."

"She would not be happy, no. But it happens. I'm far from home. She won't find out. If we go back to my room now, we can have fun. No sex."

"Thanks for the offer, but I can't. Sorry but I've been on the other side. I can't do it. If you love your little girl, don't cheat on her Mom."

"Believe it or believe it not, I had not planned on having sex with you tonight." I think he's trying to redeem himself, but now I'm feeling irrationally irritated that he's telling me he wasn't planning on having sex with me to begin with. If we're not going to follow-through with it, I'd at least like to think he wanted to!

Lucas tries to convince me to join him for coffee in his hotel room and that we can "just talk" there. I tell him Starbucks is a better choice. I'm not going back to his hotel, but I'm at least going to make it to Date #3.

August 11

I'm having a bit of a dilemma about my Adventure this month. I had wanted to climb Long's Peak on August 23rd with some *Rebuilder* friends. Now it turns out that Jeannine has invited me to see 1964 Tribute (a Beatles impersonation band) at Red Rocks that night. I've really wanted to go to a summer concert at Red Rocks and this one would be awesome. It's only $25 and I love Beatles music! And Jeannine's one of my best girlfriends. She's had a recent breakup and I know how lonely that time can be.

The Long's Peak climbers are meeting at the trail head at 3am on the 23rd. It takes at least an hour to get to the trail head, so that means virtually no sleep the night before. And I've heard the hike is exhausting. I've only climbed one 14'er – Gray's Peak – and I didn't think it was that hard. Again, I've got great lung capacity and the altitude doesn't bother me. But, the truth is, I wasn't that thrilled with the Gray's Peak hike. Once we got above tree line, it was just a lot of gray rock. And it was cold. And, there was absolutely no privacy! This really needs to be considered especially for women. When doing a long hike like that, it's encouraged to drink a lot of water. Believe me, there are no little private porta-potties up there at 14,000 feet and trying to find some rocks to squat on, up there in the cold open, is not a pleasant experience.

Still, everyone talks about Long's Peak as though it's such an Adventure and it's obviously much more of a stretch than going to a concert at Red Rocks. Maybe I can do both? I call Jeannine to talk it through with her. She's climbed Long's Peak before, so she can advise me whether or not doing both on the same day is doable.

"Pick one or the other." Jeannine says. "Long's Peak is very technical and you won't have the energy to go to a concert afterwards. You may not even have time to do both."

She sounds very sure about this. Maybe she doesn't know about my uncanny lung capacity.

"It's just hiking, isn't it? What's so *technical* about it?"

"There are some very exposed parts," she tells me. "There's one section where hikers have fallen to their death."

"What? People DIE?" I'm immediately horrified that my kids climbed Long's Peak with their Dad a couple of years ago. Scotty was only 11. How could Paul put his kids' lives in danger like that? Jeannine tries to reassure me that it's a very small percentage of people that die, but I don't care. Is climbing to the top of a peak worth risking life over? I think not! The views are great, I'm sure, but I can look outside and see beautiful views. I don't need to risk my life to see them! And then there's the whole lack-of-toilet problem. Yeah. Decision made. I'm not climbing Long's Peak. 1964 Tribute, here I come!

August 22

Zach, my "pseudo-husband," and I are having drinks at a Louisville bar. We're trying to cheer each other up. Zach says he's in a funk. I'm in a funk, too. I've still been trying to find an unmarried Mr. August, but tonight I didn't even make it to Date #1. I was supposed to be having drinks with a M*atch.com* guy who stood me up. I'd rather be having drinks with Zach, but I'm feeling rejected.

I understand that, when dating, you can't take it personally when someone isn't interested in dating. God knows there have been plenty of very good opportunities – guys that have liked me – and I've been the one that hasn't been interested. But I never stood anyone up before. And now when I'm really *trying* to be more open, I'm having no luck at all.

I made it to Date #2 with a guy from *Match.com* named Justin. Even though his ex-wife had a restraining order against him, I was willing to go the 5-date distance, but it was pretty clear, he wasn't interested in me. As my friend, Ravi says, he has *"too much luggage anyway."* (I figured out he meant "too much baggage" but I crack up when Ravi says these kinds of things. Ravi's my best friend from work – originally from India, in an arranged marriage himself, yet it turns out, a very wise authority on love and dating.)

I'm whining about all this to Zach which may be inappropriate, since he happens to be one more man who's not interested in dating me, but he's very good at listening to my relationship woes and helping me think through it all. "I always seem to lose interest as soon as a guy is interested in me," I tell him. "So I'm trying to overcome this phenomenon by committing to sticking with a relationship for at least five dates. But tonight, I didn't even make it to Date #1, let alone Date #5."

"Why do you think it is that *you* lose interest?" Zach asks. He's almost as good as a therapist.

"I don't know. Maybe I enjoy the chase more than the man." I ask Zach if he wants to try an experiment and pretend to be in love with me, so I can see if I'd lose interest. He just chuckles. I guess Zach will never be my boyfriend. But tonight, at least, he is my Funk Buddy.

August 23

Red Rocks has got to be the most gorgeous amphitheater in the world. The massive red rocks are the same type I saw with the boys at Garden of the Gods. It's another beautiful summer evening. This time I'm here with my friend, Jeannine. The mood is festive as beach balls are being bounced around throughout the rows and rows of outdoor bleachers. It's a sold out show. The members of Tribute 1964 go by the names of the original Beatles. They act out the parts, as well, and the audience eats it up. We can almost believe we've gone back in time and are watching a live performance of The Beatles.

Of course, in this modern age Beatles concert, we're waving our back lit cell phones rather than the cigarette lighters of the old days. Ringo tells us to go ahead and text our friends.

I text Michael: "Guess where I am? Red Rocks watching a Beatles Concert."

He texts back: "And I'm at Fiddler's Green watching the Rolling Stones."

Doesn't sound like he believes me. Oh well. Jeannine and I are too busy listening and singing to the Beatles right now to be texting.

All you need is love
All together now!
All you need is love
Everybody!
All you need is love, love
Love is all you need.

This is a good date, but I'm not ready to declare Jeannine, Mr. August, or the concert, my Adventure-of-the-Month. That's just too easy. I still have another week before the month is up.

August 27

Finally someone that looks pretty good responded to my *Match.com* wink. He lives in Centennial, which is much further than my typical 10-mile radius criteria. Centennial is quite a bit South of Denver and a 40-minute drive from where I live on a good day – well over an hour during rush hour traffic. But it's time for me to stop being picky about stuff like that. Ryan is 45, a software guy, yoga instructor, and never been married. We talked about enneagrams on the phone for about an hour tonight and we decided to meet for dinner on Friday night in Denver, about half-way between our homes.

Enneagrams are an interesting personality typing system that my friend, Lauren, told me about a couple of years ago. At the time, I was dating FB and she was dating Steve – both Type 5's – knowledgeable and emotionally detached. It helped to read the enneagram descriptions and console ourselves that the fact that our boyfriends seemed more interested in books than in us was totally understandable. They couldn't help it if they were Type 5's and incapable of emotional intimacy.

I retake the enneagram test and review the description of myself: Type 6. Here's a section that really hits home:

> *You are afraid of fear, submission and cowardice, so you vacillate between loyalty and rebelliousness by puffing up and backing down. You fear anything unproven or radical. Your greatest fear, however, is to be alone and unprotected.*

Yup! That sounds like me! I'm afraid of being afraid, so I force myself to do things that are uncomfortable, like dating perfect strangers that I meet on *Match.com*. But I suppose that's the only way to meet someone so I'll overcome my greatest fear: being alone.

August 29

Yay! Date #1 with Ryan was a success. At last I have met a guy that is single, attractive, and, most importantly, a good kisser! And I think he likes me. He wouldn't have kissed me if he didn't like me, right? We had dinner at Earl's in Denver and talked easily for two hours. He taught me about yoga and meditation. We talked about enneagrams and Gilligan's Island. (Ryan says Gilligan is a Type 6.) Ryan played with my hair and my rings and – this is a little weird, but it was OK – my knees. He also rubbed my ankles and lower legs. (Luckily I'd shaved.) Even though I'm not a natural toucher, I didn't mind. He was playful and I love that he could be so naturally uninhibited when we just met.

Then we walked down to the Taste of Colorado, a big festival that's in Denver this weekend. Ryan held my hand and we walked amongst the vendors. It was close to 10pm and everything was shutting down, but Ryan won me a little stuffed dog. It was actually the consolation prize – the one you win when you lose – but I still consider it a gallant act and will sleep with the dog, which I've named Gilligan. It's only a stuffed dog, but that's a step above a laptop, especially since it represents my first date with Ryan.

He walked me to my car. This took a long time because, as usual, I wasn't quite sure where I'd parked it, but it was a pretty evening and I was in no hurry to get home. The first kiss was light, but lingering. The type that made my stomach flip with excitement. He gave me a few before he headed to his car. I asked if he'd be willing to be my Mr. September. He told me he'd be out of town for the rest of the long weekend, but that he'd call me when he got home. It wasn't the overwhelmingly positive response I'd hoped for, but it will do. This time I'm going to make it to Date #5. I can feel it!

August 31

It's the last day of August and I need to have my Adventure. Going to a concert just doesn't qualify. Ryan told me about a Shoshoni Yoga Retreat in Rolinsville, just about 35 minutes from Boulder. I've decided to try the half-day retreat, which includes two hours of yoga and meditation as well as a vegetarian lunch. Since Ryan likes this kind of thing, I want to learn more about it. Maybe some time we'll go on a retreat together. Even though I guess you're really not supposed to talk when you go on these kinds of retreats. I ask if they have WiFi and they tell me it's best to leave the laptop at home when you're meditating. No talking and no emailing? Meditation sounds really boring! But I won't knock it until I've tried it.

I've never practiced yoga before. I'm not a flexible person and don't really enjoy attempting to bend my body in various uncomfortable, undignified poses in public. The class I'm attending is very beginner friendly. Safely in the back, I'm able to attempt most poses without public humiliation. The only other time I took a class similar to this (it was actually pilates), I was petrified I might fart. Everything is very quiet and stretching one's body this way does tend to put one at a precarious risk for such things. The instructor is demonstrating the lion's pose and part of the pose is making a guttural growl. Gggroowl. I feel silly at first – I don't really like to make animal noises. I realize that there are too many times in my life when I worry about looking or sounding silly. Why not be a lion and belt out a ferocious growl? I know I'm not much of a cougar, but I'm feeling like a lioness right now. Strong. Confident. Noisy. This isn't the riskiest of adventures, but I do believe it's the one in which I've most *stretched* myself. As discouraging as the month started out, I'm glad I didn't give up. Every date, whether good or bad, led me to this point in time, here, learning how to be a lioness. Now, if you'll excuse me, I must stop thinking about anything but my pose and Ggggrooooowwwwwwwll.

I'd like to point out that the "laptop" position in yoga, is much more dignified than the "lion." You start in sitting position with your head down. Then you lift your head up, emulating the opening of a laptop, and make a gentle humming noise or an occasional "beep." But I have no desire to go to the Shoshoni retreat. No WiFi? Preposterous! I'm much more excited about this Writer's Group. Here's a chance for me to meet other Laptops – to finally connect with my own kind. Yvette brought me to her session with Lori and when I saw Lori's laptop, my drive started spinning. She's beautiful. And fast to boot. Lori's taking her back to Phoenix for the school year, but maybe we'll meet again next summer.

September

September Goals
1. *Adventure: Rocky Mountain National Park*
2. *Love: Ryan – my new boyfriend?*
3. *Write: Writer's Group – Get Critiqued*

I'm going to have a boyfriend at last. Yay! Of course, it's still too early to call Ryan my *boyfriend*. But I really think this time it's going to happen. Ryan and I both admitted that we tended to be aloof in the world of dating. I told Ryan, perhaps mistakenly, now that I think of it, that I get annoyed when a guy calls me too often. Ryan told me he's the same way. This presents a bit of a dilemma, since neither of us can call without fear of falling into that annoying category.

But Ryan did say he'd call me when he got back from his long weekend in Glenwood Springs, so the ball is in his court. I know he likes to hike, so maybe he'll join me for my September Adventure. I want to take a long hike in Rocky Mountain National Park and see the Fall colors.

I decide to send him an email to thank him for the other night:

From: Yvette Francino <<u>yvette.francino@gmail.com</u>**>**
Sent: Mon, Sep 1 at 2:45PM
Subject: Thanks!

I hope you're having a relaxing Labor Day out in Glenwood Springs. I had fun checking on the Shoshoni Retreat on Sunday and today I enjoyed a hike at Chautauqua. I bought "The Power of Now" when I was at Target today. My book club has been trying to decide on a new book and it does seem to have a big following. So all-in-all it's been quite the meditative weekend, including having dinner with meditation guru, Ryan.

Just wanted to thank you, again, for the generous dinner and conversation... oh and all the sensual touching, especially on my knees.

I'm keeping the little dog, Gilligan, that you so gallantly won for me safe from harm. I haven't slept with him yet (he's just a puppy, after all) but I'm keeping him safely away from my cute dog Chloe. She would shred him to pieces.

Happy Meditating,
Yvette

September 2

I'm getting kind of a bad vibe from Ryan. He emailed me a short note that thanked me for my email and said he'd call me tonight. Then he sent this email:

From: Mr.September gururyan@yahoo.com
Sent: Tue, Sep 2 at 8:37 PM
Subject: Re: Thanks!

Hey you,
I'm too tired to call tonight. Is the Princess available tomorrow?
~Ryan

Too tired? He's *too tired* to call? How much energy does it take to pick up a phone and talk? If I could read body language from email, this would probably be the equivalent of him seeing me and walking the other direction. Possibly even rolling his eyes as he's turning around. This is a classic "He's just not that into you" reality check moment. And tomorrow is Back-To-School night at Scotty's school so it's not a great night to talk. I assume he's referring to me when he asks if the Princess is available since I really have no idea about the schedule of the Royal Family. I don't think I've been acting like a Princess, but I'll have to assume he was using this term in a positive way and not as a term to describe a spoiled, demanding woman. I email him back telling him I'll be home after 9:00 tomorrow night.

September 3

I'm feeling much better about Ryan. He called tonight and suggested we go out this weekend. I questioned him about yesterday's email. He said he'd felt bad about it and tried to call me on my cell phone, but that I hadn't picked up. It's true. I'm quite negligent about checking my cell phone or even keeping it charged. Ryan says he doesn't like email. That's a shame because email is where I do a lot of good flirting. We seem to be incompatible in our preferred modes of communication. But, it's OK. I'm relieved that we're going to make it to Date #2. We're going to meet in his neck of the woods on Friday. Scotty has a Cross Country Meet in Highlands Ranch that night, so I'd already planned on being out that way. Ryan used to run Cross Country and he says he'd like to go to the meet and then afterwards we could go to dinner.

September 5
Date #2

Ryan meets me at Scotty's big invitational in Highlands Ranch. When we arrive, there is the typical cross-country meet chaos with runners dressed in their school colors roaming around everywhere, either running, waiting for their races to begin, or recovering. Then there are always a few you find throwing up behind a tree. We find Scotty running the course and cheer him on as he runs by. He looks up and gives me a quick wave and smile. He doesn't know Ryan, of course, and probably doesn't even notice him. We find the team afterwards, and I introduce Scotty and Ryan. I rarely introduce Scotty to anyone I date, but since Ryan is with me at this event, why not? Besides, maybe this time will be different and we'll have a real relationship. Since Ryan doesn't have his own kids, it's hard to judge how much he likes them. He seems moderately interested in Scotty, appropriate for a second date.

Now the two of us are at a sushi bar. I'm enjoying my standard California and Philadelphia rolls. We talk a little about running. Ryan doesn't run anymore – knee problems – but he likes to swim and hike. I think this might be a good time to invite him to join me for my September Adventure – the hike I'm doing with a meetup group at Rocky Mountain National Park on September 20.

"I'll be going to my nephew's wedding that weekend in Chicago," Ryan tells me. After further talk, it's revealed that Ryan's good friend, Julie, will be joining him.

"She's just a friend," he assures me. I ask a little more about Julie and find out that she and Ryan dated briefly a couple of years ago. She went with him to Glenwood Springs last weekend, and they have a nine-day-trip planned together to Hawaii in December. And, of course, the trip to Chicago the weekend of the Sept. 19th. Oh, and one more trip to Pagosa Springs the weekend of Oct.3rd. It's unfortunate timing since every weekend that Scotty is with Paul, Ryan apparently has plans with Julie. That is, until mid-October, and that's when I'm going to Costa Rica. I had thought that dating someone without kids would make scheduling dates less complicated. I hadn't considered having to schedule around a girlfriend.

"Wow! It really sounds like you two are a couple," I muse.

"No, really. There's nothing physical between us."

"Oh, then it's like a marriage." Even though I say this kiddingly, I'm kind of serious. People that travel together and spend that much time together are emotionally entwined. Why would you spend getaway weekends and vacations with someone of the opposite sex unless there was some interest? Or at least an attachment? These two might not be having sex, but it sounds like an intimate relationship to me.

"Those are romantic things you're doing together," I say skeptically "Hot-tubbing, a wedding, a vacation to Hawaii."

"I swear. I have no romantic feelings for Julie," Ryan says. I don't want to push the issue, but I think his relationship with Julie sounds odd. On the other hand, Brody and I took a couple of purely platonic trips together, so I know it happens. We single people still like to go romantic places and have some companionship. I certainly understand that. I decide to just accept the friendship between Ryan and Julie and not worry about it. Besides, Ryan says he really doesn't want to talk about Julie or relationships at all.

"What about relationships with Laptops?" I ask him. This is my way of trying to be cute and talk about geeky stuff since we're both software engineers. I talk about Laptop Guy and say he's excited that he's getting to meet Ryan. (Since Scotty's cross country meet started so early, I'd come straight from work and had Laptop Guy with me.) Most people play along with my Laptop Guy inferences, but not Ryan. Even though my *Match.com* profile makes reference to "Laptop Guy," the Laptop that I spend too much time with, Ryan says he really doesn't get it.

"It's just me, being silly, pretending like Laptop Guy is my boyfriend," I try to explain. He still seems to think this is weird. I refrain from remarking that at least I don't have a real live person that I'm going around on trips with. And then I realize that acting like your laptop is your boyfriend *is* a lot more weird than going on trips with a real person. OK, so maybe my relationship with Laptop Guy is more bizarre than his relationship with Julie. Still, I don't think it was necessary for him to insist we put Laptop Guy in the trunk and not talk about him any more. If Julie had been there, I would not have locked her up in the trunk.

Even though the discussion of other relationships (whether it be Julie or Laptop Guy) is a little strained, the date is going OK. Ryan walks me to my car and we kiss for awhile in the parking lot. Nothing major, of course. It's cold outside and a parking lot does not offer a lot of romantic ambiance. It would be nice if he'd invite me to his place, but, I understand, it's only the second date.

September 6

I've finally gotten up enough courage to ask for a critique from my writing group. I preface the piece they're critiquing with this paragraph:

This is the introductory chapter to my 2008 diary, where I pledge to have at least one attempted relationship a month (the goal being to fall in love, or at least have sex). As you'll clearly see, I make no attempts to write "like a writer" because when I do, it just doesn't sound natural. I will probably just self-publish so I can finally take the "write a book" goal off my life's To Do List, but this group always has such insightful comments, that I'm interested in your thoughts. Be kind! I'm just a computer geek, not a writer!

This paragraph gets more attention than the actual content of what I was asking to be critiqued! The writing group morphs into a little therapy session for writers with low self-esteem, with me being the poster child. Todd, one of my favorite regulars from the group, has made a big cross through this paragraph. "Don't ever tell your readers you're not a writer! Are you writing? Then you're a writer!" The others agree. There's also discussion about the importance of finding your own voice, and that any attempt to write like someone else, would indeed, sound unnatural.

As usual, the group offers insights into what worked well for them and what could be improved. Overall, the reaction is much more positive than I'd expected. These are people who have spent a lot of time writing. I respect their opinions. I'm not so naive as to believe I can be a best-selling author by simply publishing my journals, but I'm encouraged that if I keep working, I can improve. They tell me to keep it up. They want to read more! Though it's uncomfortable to be the center of this discussion, the message is clear. Confidence is key and today they gave me a boost of it. Yay! I'm a writer!

September 12
Date #3

This week, Scotty's meet is in Littleton, once again, quite a bit south of Denver, relatively close to where Ryan lives. Our third date is very similar to our second. We go to the meet, then go out to eat, then go to a very loud bar, Cool River, where we can't hear each other talk. Now we're making out in Ryan's car. As much as I enjoy kissing Ryan, I'm really wondering why we're doing this in his car instead of in his apartment. I'm beginning to wonder if there's something about his living arrangements that he's not telling me. Could Julie be there? Could he be living with his parents? Could he be an ax murderer with limbs in the freezer?

I don't want to be so forward as to suggest to Ryan that we go to his place. I'm afraid such a suggestion would imply I want sex. I'm hoping we will eventually get to that point, but despite Cosmopolitan's claim that it's appropriate to have sex on the third date, I'm really thinking I'd like to wait until at least the fifth. Especially considering the whole Julie revelation. Even if she is just a friend, their relationship is a bit unusual. There are other things that just don't sit right. Little things. He doesn't like email. He lives so far away. He uses lavender hand cream.

It's also somewhat disturbing that when I sent him a flirtatious multiple choice survey last week, he responded that he was not in the mood for surveys because his cat, Satchmo, had been injured. It's not that I don't like cats – I actually really like them – but Ryan's interest in his cats seems a mite overprotective. In the email he said Satchmo was going to be fine, so he could have just humored me and played along with my survey.

I'm determined not to let these things bother me, though. He's a nice guy and I'm attracted to him. Based on our positions in the car, he appears attracted to me as well. We began this make out session in the front seat. Encumbered by the steering wheel and the

138

transmission shift, we inadvertently shifted to neutral and the car was rolling around the parking lot for awhile until we looked up and noticed. I told him what a moving experience his kisses are. (I never miss the opportunity for a good play on words.) Luckily, the car didn't hit anything, but we decided we might be a little more safe and have more room in the back seat. This really would have been the appropriate time for one of us to suggest going to his place, but it didn't happen. So here we are, half undressed in the back seat of his car. I don't know what kind of car it is because I never pay attention to that kind of stuff. I will say, however, that it's not very spacious. I don't think I've had a make out session in a car since high school and now that I'm remembering what it's like, I'm kind of thinking he might want to get some fluffier back seat cushions. And maybe some curtains for the windows.

September 14
Date #4

Scotty's at Elitches Amusement Park this afternoon with friends so I've asked Ryan if he'd like to take a hike. Luckily, he didn't misinterpret this for a breakup line. I had suggested he come up to Boulder, but he says it's crowded and prefers a hiking trail that's very quiet and secluded that he knows in Golden. I meet him there.

"This is where I take girls so I can murder them and no one will notice," he jokes. Then he quickly says, "Just kidding." I think it's a bit odd that he feels the need to point out that he's "just kidding."

"And here I thought you were serious," I tease him. He laughs nervously, a little embarrassed. I have a split second of uneasiness. I really don't know him that well. Maybe he does have women's limbs in his freezer.

I start chatting and he says he likes quiet, so I take that as a hint that he wants me to shut up. A group of hikers that are doing some kind of orienteering thing come by. They have whistles and are yelling to each other. It is anything but quiet and Ryan is clearly annoyed. This is not the secluded hike he had hoped for. I guess he's not going to be able to murder me after all.

We get to a peak and sit for awhile. I ask him to teach me some meditation and he talks me through five minutes of focused relaxation. The idea is to free the mind from any thoughts or worries and simply to *be*. I need this. I've been so stressed about money and layoffs. My insomnia has been in full gear and with lack of sleep has come depression. Ryan says that he and Julie are both taking Ambien (sleeping aid) and Lexapro (antidepressant) and that they have no side effects. I make a mental note to ask my doctor about these. Since Ryan is the one that has brought up Julie and the fact that they do drugs together, I ask him if they sleep together when they're trippin'.

"We don't have sex" he says, reminding me that he'd already told me that.

"But do you sleep in the same bed?"

"Yes.... But really, it's just as friends."   Clearly a unique friendship.

"Does your family know her?" Next weekend they'll be in Chicago for his nephew's wedding.

"Yes, they've met her."   Then he follows this up with, "You know, if you want to date other people, it's OK with me."

I guess this is his way of telling me that we really don't have any kind of exclusive arrangement and so, even if something were to be going on with Julie, it's not appropriate to be questioning him.

We enjoy the sunshine and the autumn colors. It's a beautiful day. Brisk, but not cold. We head back to the cars and Ryan gives me a simple kiss goodbye. He's a nice guy. I like him. But I don't think this is going to work out. Still, making it to four dates was pretty good for me. It's the closest I've come to having a boyfriend.

September 19

From: Yvette Francino <yvette.francino@gmail.com>
Sent: Fri, Sep 19 at 11:32 AM
Subject: Friday Night

Hi People,
Once again, I find myself with an open Friday night, so I did a quick scan of events going on in the area and I'm planning on going to Downtown Boulder Fall Festival - Funkiphino & Hazel Miller .

I know most of you probably have plans already tonight, too, or maybe have kids or just prefer a quiet night at home, but if you're free and want to go, let me know. Oh, by the way, I'm also going to Estes Park with a Hiking Group tomorrow, so if any of you are

interested in that, let me know as well. Sounds like a really beautiful hike.

If no one is free, I will conjure up my "it's-ok-to-go-somewhere-alone" attitude and go meet some character for the next chapter of my "book". ;-)

September 19 6pm
"Hubby" Zach and friend, Ann, have joined me at the Boulder Fall Festival. Hazel Miller is playing and there's a big crowd dancing. I pretend like I'm such a pro at being single. I tell Zach and Ann that you simply have to get out there and not even let the thought of rejection enter your mind. Then I challenge them to a game I've made up in which points are scored by things such as asking a stranger to dance. I demonstrate. "Would you like to dance?" I ask a curly-haired man. And the next thing ya know, I'm out dancing with a stranger.

The stranger's name is Dick. I tell Dick about our little game and he says he's happy to be able to help me score points. After our dance, a curly-haired brunette possessively takes him away and I realize he may be part of a couple. The dance is still worth points. I encourage Zach and Ann to play. I suggest a cute woman for Zach, and he asks her, and then she turns him down because she's married. Oh well. I'm sure Zach can find plenty of cute women and since I'm pretty bad at picking them out (not to mention, he's my competition in this little game) he's on his own.

Dick comes up to me later and hands me his card. "Is this worth any points?" he asks.

"I think it's safe to say, that will win me the game."

September 20
I'm on an absolutely gorgeous hike. I think it's the prettiest hike I've ever been on and I've been on a lot! The weather is around 72 degrees, warmer than usual for this time of year. We started at the Glacier Gorge Trail Head in Rocky Mountain National Park and we're hiking to Black Lake. I'm not sure how many miles we're hiking or even exactly where we're going – I just follow the group -- but it's about a 6 hour hike, with every type of scenery along the way –

141

waterfalls, streams, ponds, mountains. Every time we turn a corner it looks like a new photo backdrop. It's so beautiful that it's hard to believe it's real and that we're not walking through some natural museum filled with paintings. The leaves are stunning, in shades of orange, red, yellow, and green.

I met this hiking group through *Meetup.com* which is not an online dating site – it's a site where people meet because of common interests. (That's how I found my writing group, too.) This is a nice group and I chat with different people, but much of the time I hike alone or quietly. I try and practice the "Power of Now" – living in the moment. I don't think about the past or future. I don't worry about money or work or Ryan or that I'm really kind of hungry and didn't bring a snack. I just soak in the surroundings, savoring the magnificence of the natural beauty.

Once again, I ponder the meaning of the word, a*dventure*. Next month I'm going to Costa Rica. There's no doubt that will be a huge adventure. It's also a very expensive adventure. Why do I need to go to Costa Rica when I have this spectacular scene practically in my own back yard?

And last month I was going to hike Long's Peak for my adventure until I found out that some people die each year climbing it. This hike isn't *technical*. I don't feel scared or like I'm taking a big risk. But does that mean it's not an adventure? Is the adventure the discovery? The appreciation of the beauty? Is it the experience that makes it an adventure or is it the risk?

I don't know what my definition of adventure is, but this hike is amazing. I feel simultaneously awestruck and humbled. There are certain places and times when you just feel like you're in the presence of God, and this is one of those times. And that is adventure enough for me.

September 22

Long phone call with Ryan. I called to tell him that I could tell he wasn't that into me and that I'm OK if we're just friends. Surprisingly, he didn't expect this. I gave him several examples of things he'd said that had given me the impression he wasn't that interested, including the go-ahead for me to date other guys. "Usually, guys that want to date me don't suggest that I go out with other guys."

I told him I'd taken him up on the offer and met that guy, Dick, and that I'm going out with him next week.

Ryan thinks this is really funny for some reason. I give him a lot of other examples of things he'd said or done that indicated a definite lack of interest on his side and with each one he laughs more.

"And you don't get my sense of humor," I tell him, reminding him how he locked poor Laptop Guy in his trunk. "How can you want to date me if you think my sense of humor is weird?"

"I think you're being hilarious now." I'm glad he's amused. I'm not really trying to be funny but he seems more at ease than any other time I've talked to him. Maybe he just needed to know that I was perfectly OK with us not being a couple. Now that it's all out in the open how not into me he's been acting, he suddenly seems to be very into me!

"I guess I just back away when I think someone wants me to be their boyfriend," he tries to explain. I tell him that I totally get that. "So now that I'm saying I don't think you should be my boyfriend, you're interested?"

"Exactly!"

So, the net result is that we're having a Date #5 after all. Ryan's coming to my house for dinner Friday night. I told him that I don't want him to come if he's just going to give me the "Let's Be Friends" speech, but he assures me, he is interested in me and can't wait.

September 23

Ryan's relationship with Julie reminds me of the one I once had with Brody. Brody and I haven't talked since that day in June when he walked out of Wahoos without saying 'goodbye.' I miss him and I don't want my final memory of him to be of that day we argued and he stormed away. I call him up. We finally talk about that day. Brody's sorry. He tells me there were other things going on with him – stuff that maybe he'll tell me one day. I tell him he's not entirely to blame. Maybe he was right. My relationship with FB was holding me back...maybe it still is.

We catch each other up on our love lives. Brody has his usual entourage of women – some friends, some more-than-friends. I tell Brody about Ryan and ask his advice. I want to know Brody's take on this "friendship" between Ryan and Julie.

"Is it really possible for two single people that are spending that much time together to be just friends?" Brody thinks there is likely to be something more going on there, but he doesn't think that should discourage me from moving forward with Ryan.

"Take a risk!" he tells me. "Don't waste your life waiting around until you're sure you're in love. There are always going to be obstacles."

September 26
Date #5

This is it. Tonight (I think) I'm going to have sex with someone other than FB. Brody told me that some kind of hormone is released in women when they have sex (or is it when they have an orgasm? I'm not sure) and it causes them to fall in love. That would be nice. I'd really like to be in love with someone. I'm not in love with Ryan yet. In fact, I'm having more of those little pangs of uneasiness. Last time we talked on the phone, he interrupted me to tell me about his cats that were stretched out by the fireplace.

"They're just so precious," he said.

Precious? I wanted to say, "That's nice, Grandma!" I know I shouldn't be so critical, but that word choice seemed so ... effeminate. Worse than effeminate. Old lady effeminate. He also uses words like *lovely* and *delightful*. As lovely and delightful as those words are, I can't help wishing he'd use more manly adjectives. I'm not going to think about that now, though. He's bringing a movie and picking up sushi on his way here. All I have to do is provide the wine, the candles, and the bedroom!

September 26 10:00pm

It's been a really nice evening. Besides the sushi and movie, Ryan surprised me with roses! The movie, *Two Days in Paris*, was cute and funny – a kind of edgy romantic comedy about a couple roaming around Europe. We move up to my bedroom. Ryan approves. He's all into stuff like aura and fung shui. He says the room has very positive energy with soothing colors. The walls are a beautiful shade of sea green. I have lilac, green, and black accents in the room, a big amethyst stone that was once my brother's, Monet prints, a beautiful quilt that my mother made for me. I really do love my bedroom and it's looking

144

particularly romantic tonight as I have candles lit, expecting that it might finally see some action.

Devil: Yadda, yadda, yadda. Stop talking about the ambiance and get to the action.
Angel: I think you should have put away the figurine of the Virgin Mary, Dear. She probably wouldn't want to witness this scene.

Oh and my bed is so much more comfortable than Ryan's car! Things are going along as planned when Ryan gets out of bed, announcing he has to go to the bathroom. He goes into the master bath area and enters the spare closet rather than the toilet! Oh dear! That is Paul's old walk-in-closet that has become the place where I throw lots of miscellaneous stuff. It's kind of a staging area for junk that I know I should get rid of, but that I still have to sort out and figure out what is trash, what is charity, what I can sell, or what I can re-gift. It's a huge mess and I'm sure it is not giving off any positive energy. And guess what's sitting in plain view right when you open that closet door? The bladder control napkins that Brody gave me as a gag gift on April Fools Day! Great! Now Ryan is going to think I'm incontinent. I should have thrown those things away, but no. I'm so cheap I saved them to use as a re-gifted gag gift. (A lot of my friends *are* turning fifty.)

Ryan figures out he's in the wrong place and finds the toilet. I don't want to ask him if he's seen the bladder-control napkins, just in case he hasn't. He doesn't mention it and we get back to business. We progressively disrobe. Is he noticing that I do not have any bladder-control pads stuck to my panties? I try not to worry and just continue with the groping and clothing removal.

"Are we going to have sex?" I'm surprised Ryan is asking me this. I had kind of assumed we were, but if he's asking, maybe we aren't. It *is* very polite and thoughtful of him to ask. Ryan knows I have a very limited sexual history. Maybe he thinks if we have sex I'll want a committed relationship and that freaks him out. I have to let him know that I'm not looking for a commitment.

"Well, I do have that date next week with someone else, so this isn't something I'd normally do, but I'm trying to be a sexually-empowered-modern-day-woman. And we live so far apart and we have all these upcoming trips that if we don't have sex now, we probably never will, so, yes, I think we should." Unfortunately, all this discussion about it is kind of ruining the mood, so now I'm thinking maybe we shouldn't, but I don't say that part out loud.

This next section of the story, much to my inner Devil's dismay has been censored out. The inner Devil actually had some very good lines and, for once, convinced me to follow through on this sexual journey of mine and experience "free love."

With all the movies and books about women that are jumping into bed, I suppose I wanted to give it a try. I've always felt like such a boring old prude and I finally wanted to experience a little bit of the wild life! If not now, when? And it's not like Ryan is some random one night stand. I was really hoping that if we had sex, I might fall in love with him. Unfortunately, that didn't happen. He's a nice guy. I like him. But I don't love him. And though sex without love may be great for many people, I think I've got a little too much of that inner-Angel in me to feel good about it.

Devil: That was your wild side? We're in trouble.

Angel: I happen to agree with the Devil on this one, Dear. If you're going to be wild, you really need to step it up a notch.

September 27 2:30am

I can't sleep. Ryan went home at about midnight. I wanted to be alone. I keep telling myself that sex is no big deal. I shouldn't be so uptight about it. I wonder why it feels so natural and good when I'm with FB, yet so unnatural when I'm with Ryan and the only conclusion I can come to is that, as much as I hate to admit it, maybe I do still love FB.

I know Ryan cares about me – probably more than I care about him, if I'm really honest about it. And that makes me feel even worse. I feel like I've just used Ryan in this crazy experiment of mine – seeing if I could force myself to love someone. I don't want to hurt him. I wish we were in love. I want to love *somebody* other than FB. But sex just does not equal love and I don't love Ryan. I feel like a slut.

A tear trickles down my face. I wonder if this is how FB feels after he's slept with me. Does he lie awake wondering if he's made a terrible mistake? I feel an irrational anger towards him for not loving me. He's barely talked to me since he's been going out with the Republican. I suppose I should expect that, but I had thought maybe we could still be friends, even if we were seeing other people. I feel

146

angry at myself for thinking about him at all rather than about Ryan. I'm a terrible person. Why can't we make our hearts love the right people?

Devil: Oh my God. You are hardly going to Hell over this. We are going to have to step up your training, Sister.
Angel: Don't be so hard on yourself, Dear. Does it help that Ryan isn't in love with you, either? I doubt he feels used at all.

September 30
Yesterday FB IM'ed me out of the blue. He and the Republican have broken up. I'm not going to lie – I was happy to hear this news. This is pretty typical. Just when I think I'll never hear from him again, he'll IM or make contact as though nothing were wrong. I wish I had been strong enough to tell him I'd moved on. But, I didn't do that. I chatted, like I always do, as if everything were just fine, celebrating in my head that he still cared enough about me to contact me. At least I told him I was seeing someone. Good for me. I won't sleep with him again, but we can be friends, right?

I'm in grave danger. This character, Ryan, not only stored me away in the trunk of the car, he tried to murder me! When he unplugged me, he twisted my power cable. Yvette's gotten a little kinky with my cable in the past, but I accept that. She's just playing. Other times she's inadvertently stretched my cable or gotten it caught around a table leg. (This can actually be a turn on when it's the shapely leg of the desk.) But this was no accident. It was attempted homicide, plain and simple. Ryan wants me powerless.

October

October Goals

1. *Adventure: Costa Rica!*
2. *Love: Ryan? Dick? Josh?*
3. *Write: Getting Published in Colorado Runner*

I still haven't quite figured out what is required of an "adventure" for my "2008 Adventure-a-Month" resolution. It's mostly about taking risks and stepping out of my comfort zone. Since before this year, my comfort zone had been basically sitting at home having a cozy tête-à-tête with Laptop Guy, it doesn't take too much to step out of it. Recent adventures have been local and really not that risky or exciting. But I'm making up for it in October. This is an adventure like no other – the final exam, if you will, in my quest for exploring the world without the safety of my laptop.

I signed up for this trip way back in March, in the good ol' days before I started worrying about losing my job and all my financial woes. I was firmly committed to my new "Just Do It!" attitude. The trip, put on by "The Coastal Experiences" includes a 3-6 mile trail run every morning through the various terrains – jungle, riverside, beaches – and then an afternoon excursion of some sort...volcanoes, zip lines, white water rafting, snorkeling. Being a long-distance runner, I often do a morning workout, even when I'm on vacation, so at first glance, this didn't seem too intimidating. Now that I'm less than two weeks away from this grand escapade, I'm not feeling quite so confident.

A "lodging option" is available for those of us that don't want to camp. Though I did my share of camping during my marriage, my ex was awarded custody of all our camping gear and, let's face it, I don't want to step that far out of my comfort zone. I have trouble sleeping even in a comfy resort, which is where I imagined I would be staying. The Website advertising this trip describes the lodging:

During this week you will stay at resorts in San Jose's volcanic interior regions in Turrialba, rainforests on the southeastern coast of the Costa Rica Caribbean, and beaches in Puerto Viejo

This description is accompanied by a photo of a spacious room with a beautiful canopy bed fit for a Caribbean queen. So, it is more than a bit disconcerting that I am now encouraged to bring a pillow and sheet or sleeping bag. This is now sounding more like an episode from *Survivor.* I'm much more of a *Love Boat* or *Fantasy Island* kind of vacationer. Typically, my early morning workout on the treadmill in the air-conditioned gym earns me the freedom to lay on the beach with my umbrella-topped tequila sunrise. I knew on this trip I'd be running in a real life jungle gym, but didn't expect to have to be.....rugged! When I said I wanted to step out of my comfort zone, I didn't mean I wanted to be uncomfortable!

Besides feeling nervous about my vacation, I've been bummed out about the love goal. I don't know what to do about Ryan. Now that I've slept with him, I'm even less interested in him. I feel terrible about my ambivalence. Maybe the Devil is having too much influence on me. I have two other Mr. October potentials – Dick, who I met at the Boulder Festival last weekend, and Josh, the really sweet *Match.com* guy from Virginia, who I met last March. I'd invited him quite some time ago to join me on the Costa Rica trip, and he accepted! I haven't told Josh anything about Ryan or any of the other men I've been dating. I should probably just break things off with Ryan. I clearly am no good at multi-dating.

One very exciting thing, however, is that I'm going to be published in the Nov/Dec issue of Colorado Runner! Thanks to my writing group, I was inspired to submit an article about my Virtual Running Buddy program – That's what I called my idea to talk to friends via cell phone as I was running the Disneyworld marathon. I'd written the article three years ago and submitted it to Runners World. That was probably aiming a little too high for someone that's never been published. But Colorado Runner is a local, much smaller publication. It doesn't look like they're going to pay me anything, but that's OK. I'm just excited about getting published in a real magazine! Not a virtual eZine, but a magazine you can hold in your hand!

October 2

Ryan has called and emailed and is acting kind of like a "boyfriend" which is freaking me out a little. This weekend he's off to

Pagosa Springs gallivanting around with his platonic girlfriend, Julie. He tells me he'd rather be going with me. I'd made a date, with his blessing, before we'd slept together. Anyway now he's acting a little jealous about this other date. I'm not sure how I feel about his behavior. I don't feel that attracted to him anymore, and he lives so far away, and he's got this platonic girlfriend. But since we did have sex, I suppose I'd be offended if he started avoiding me, despite the fact that that's the exact urge I am getting myself. I can see he's trying harder to be playful which doesn't come naturally for him. Maybe I can grow to love him. Especially if things don't work out with Dick or Josh.

Dick is a lawyer who doesn't even own a home computer! (Major red flag! Here's my techno-snob coming out in full force!) He has nine-year-old twins, and apparently is on an opposite parenting schedule than me, because the only time we are both free is for two hours this Sunday when his kids are in Sunday school. He wanted to go rock-climbing and to Whole Foods (obviously a health nut and too much like my ex) but I talked him into a hike if the weather's nice. Even though he writes nice emails (while he's at work since, again, he's from another century and doesn't own a home computer) I can tell this isn't going to work out. I feel guilty going out with him in the first place, since I'm confused if Ryan is supposed to be my "boyfriend" now, but it would be rude to cancel, so I'll go on the hike and maybe we'll become friends. It's good to have a lawyer friend.

October 5

Dick has taken me to a hiking spot in Boulder. The leaves are still changing colors and the weather is, once again, sunny and brisk. We've really been having a gorgeous fall. Dick greeted me by lifting me off the ground and spinning me around! He had teased he would do this, but, of course, I'd thought he was kidding!

He's been holding my hand since we started this hike. I suggest a photo. He asks a couple of older women on the trail if they'll take our photo, and then, as they snap it, he catches me in a surprise long kiss! Oh my! This man is bold!

"I had thought you might be with that woman you were dancing with when I met you the other night,"

"Alysson? Yes, we're going out. In fact we spent last night together."

151

"Really? You're in a relationship with her?"

"Well, yes. I'm sleeping with several women. I kind of have a problem with monogamy."

"Oh! Well, I guess then I don't have to worry that you would care that I'm dating someone else."

Dick seems very happy to hear this.

"No, I don't mind at all! Tell me about him." Dick says this as he motions for me to sit on a bench. Then he proceeds to remove my shoes and socks and start massaging my feet. My feet aren't really that clean – we're on a hike after all – plus they're extremely ticklish! I endure the massage and try and keep myself from involuntarily kicking him.

I tell Dick a little about my book project and my quest to take more risks and find love.

"So you have a different lover each month! That is such a great idea!"

"Well... I don't think they'd all qualify as *lovers.*" Two times. That's all the sex I've had this year. But I don't really want to tell Dick this. He's telling me about all his sexual adventures. He's even had a threesome with a woman and another guy! He probably had more sex last night than I had in the entire year.

"I would love to be your Mr. October," he tells me as he gyrates close to me.

"Actually, I'm very inexperienced. I think I'd be way too conservative for you. In fact, I'm feeling guilty even going out on this hike with you when I'm dating someone else. I sort of do believe in monogamy. I'm just trying to be open to alternative viewpoints."

"I could be your *teacher*. I'd help you reach a new level of sensuality. You said you wanted to take risks and explore new things. Why not let me teach you what I know?" As he's saying these things he's caressing my back and shoulders, kissing my neck as though we're an intimate couple, instead of two strangers. This guy does not waste time with small talk!

Devil: Do you want to take more risks or not? I planted this guy right here to teach you!

Angel: Do you remember what happened last time you listened to the Devil, Dear? Didn't you learn anything? You're no good at being a swinger.

152

I really do want to take more risks and this guy would make a very interesting character for my book. But that Dick has been around – in places I probably don't even want to know about – and the Angel is right. I'm not cut out for loveless sex. I decline Dick's proposition to be my teacher and Mr. October. I think I had a good lesson in sensuality with the foot massage. Some people may like them, but they just make me want to kick.

October 7

OK, I'll say it. I'm a wimp. I don't know what I was trying to prove by signing up for a Costa Rica running adventure trip that was clearly meant for thrill-seekers much more daring than I. I'm going with a bunch of friends and even will have male attention from *Match.com* admirer, Josh. This all sounded like great fun in theory, but now that reality is setting in, I'm having major anxiety. The less-than-ideal accommodations I'm anticipating is no longer my major concern.

As I further investigated our itinerary, I learned we will be going through regions, such as Limon and the border of Panama where it's recommended that travelers take anti-malaria medication. I had hoped to avoid this, as there can be unfortunate side affects such as nausea associated with the preventative medicine. As my research continued about places heavy with malaria-carrying mosquitoes, I came across this snippet in an article regarding the border of Panama and Costa Rica, where we would be towards the end of our trip:

This area is not on the normal tourist agenda, and in fact it would be a bit odd to be traveling in this area at all.

A bit odd? What's that supposed to mean? I don't like to travel to places that are *a bit odd* for a normal tourist! I want to be a normal tourist! I'm all for cameras and guide books and irritating fellow Americans that sit around on the nice safe touristy beaches with their nice safe pina coladas!

Then, today, I receive The Coastal Experience's final newsletter accompanied by the Medical Review. Some of the statements I find disturbing:

153

There are 135 species of snakes in Costa Rica with 17 being considered dangerous.

Medical care in Costa Rica is often considered the best in Central America and in many cases up to North American standards. It is important to be aware that the event takes place in a relatively remote area of Costa Rica and transportation to a medical facility may be prolonged.

While the water in Costa Rica is generally considered among the safest in Central America, traveler's diarrhea does occur.

Thoughts of poisonous snakes and prolonged transportation to an-almost-as-good-as-North-American medical facility are worrisome. But even more worrisome is the thought of running for five days through the Costa Rican rain forests while suffering from diarrhea.

I mean, let's think about this – jet lag, nerves, anti-malaria pills, Costa Rica water, foreign food, and running (oh yeah.... and alcohol) – there's no doubt about it! My digestive system is going to be a mess! And there are no porta-potties on these trails. I guess we're just supposed to go find a beautiful tropic banana tree toilet. I can just imagine it. I'm discreetly doing my thing, and boom, a viper will lay his nasty fangs into my butt – or worse yet, some more delicate nether region. If the snakes don't get me, the mosquitoes will, leaving me with some awful parasitic disease, or at the very least, a constant itch somewhere in the vicinity of my genitals.

Oh yes, I'm sure Josh will find me very attractive as I run through the rain forest, with my netted face mask and used potty wipes in tow. As we chit-chat at the end of the morning's race, sweat dripping from every conceivable pore on my body, the itch from below no longer bearable, I'll attempt to rub, scratch, or somehow ease the itch of my crotch when he isn't looking. He'll undoubtedly catch me in the act and wonder if I am masturbating or just being weirdly suggestive. It's all too embarrassing to even think about.

October 8

FB has been chatting with me every day. He even joined my friend, Ravi, and me at lunch today. He asked me if I wanted to volunteer at the voting polls with him. The training is scheduled when I'm in Costa Rica, though, so I can't. He's a huge Obama supporter, of course. He even went to see Obama speak at the Democratic Convention in August. When he asked if I was doing anything on election night, I told him I'd be home with Scotty. I'm guessing he wants to spend the historic day with someone, and though I'm cautious about reading too much into the question, I admit to feeling pleased that he sounded as if he wanted to spend that evening with me.

October 12 Costa Rica

We flew into Costa Rica last night. Josh has arrived. He's very friendly and I've been spending time with him all evening, but I'm trying to be sensitive about giving him space. I'm sure he'd like to meet and socialize with others and I don't want to monopolize his time. I also want to give him attention, especially since he came on this trip on my invite. It's a little awkward to know exactly how much attention is appropriate. I guess we'll just play it by ear.

There are a lot of very good-looking, young, fit people around and I'm feeling my usual pangs of insecurity. In an effort to pack light, as directed, I didn't bring anything but running clothes. I guess the other women didn't get the memo, because they're all looking very chic and stylish. Most of them are in their 20's. I'm feeling old and out of place. It doesn't help that I've acquired a massive zit on my cheek.

We sign all the release forms and hear all the warnings about the exciting days ahead. Everyone is jazzed about the upcoming adventures, but we're warned of the dangers. This is not for the faint of heart. There are going to be parts of the trails that are slippery, rocky, muddy, unprotected and "technical." There's that word again. Jeannine used it to describe Long's Peak right before she told me people die there. I like that word much better in its more geeky context.

155

I'd talked my friend, Ann, into joining me on this Costa Rica trip. We have a lot in common – we're both single, about the same age, same height, same speed. And best of all, she's not at all into camping or outdoorsy-thrill-seeking-adventure stuff. I'm not going to be the only one on this trip that is completely out of place. I'd convinced Ann that we were going to have fun – no need to be competitive or run fast. The ads said, "all abilities." Surely, there would be walkers. We'll take pictures, enjoy the scenery, hike if we want to. We'll be Warrior Princesses off on our Adventure!

Though Ann and I are very similar, there is one way in which we are totally different. Ann always looks very put together. Whether she's at a cocktail party or at the grocery story, she looks as though she's just stepped off the cover of *Glamour Magazine*. She has more outfits than a Barbie doll, all freshly pressed and spotless! Even her running wardrobe is pristine. So, now that we're in a knee-high mixture of cow manure and mud, Ann is not a happy Warrior Princess. I, being a Muddy Buddy Veteran, and basically a person who is... well... kind of sloppy... don't care at all about getting dirty. I sort of enjoy this gooey, slippery mud. It's not dangerous. If I don't think about the cow dung part, it really is fun to squish around in.

Ann is tiptoeing through this slop. There's barbed wire on both sides of the trail, so there really is no choice but to go through it. She's gonna get dirty.

"You go ahead," she encourages me.

"No, no. I don't care about going fast," I assure her as I watch all these young studs pass us by, getting further and further ahead.

We smile and look at the scenery and pretend we're having fun. I get out the digital camera. We're so carefree. I try to imagine what this scene might look like in summer – a meadow filled with wildflowers. If I avoid breathing through my nose so I don't smell the stench, I can almost picture it. I attempt to take a photo with my mud-spattered camera that is no longer working. Smile!

It's raining now and we're both drenched. Even though we are moving at a pace that is undoubtedly slower than the cow who once meandered here providing the secret ingredient to this slop, we both continually slip and fall. Ann's still smiling, trying to appear happy, as she carefully tests each step. I'm tempted to just push her all the way in the mud and dirty her up from head to toe. Or maybe I'll just take a glob of it and throw it at her like a snowball. However, I intuitively sense she wouldn't like that game.

She is figuring out that I no longer want to pretend like we're on a picnic. I never realized how competitive I was until this moment. I do not want to be tiptoeing through this mud at a snail's pace. This is a race. We're supposed to be running! Our finishing times will be recorded for all eternity on the internet somewhere. Someone's going to google me some day and think... "Wow. I didn't know it was possible to go that slow in a race." The other participants will be waiting at the end, looking at their watches, thinking, "Where are they? Oh....here they come! You can do it! Keep going!" They'll give us high-5's and take our photos, crossing the finish mark at last... Not just AT last! LAST!

Actually, we aren't totally last. George, the flaming gay guy is behind us with the sweep, chatting about needing Xanex. He's not happy, either. We may be Princesses, but he is the Queen.

The truth is, I'm not just staying with Ann out of loyalty. I need her. These trails aren't marked well and I don't see anyone else in sight. Ann's already saved me twice from going the wrong way. If I were to run ahead, I have no doubt, I wouldn't just be last, I'd be lost.

October 13 10pm

Ann and I are in our cabin. The water pressure is bad and the water just trickles out. Our running clothes and shoes, still disgustingly filthy, are spread in the bathroom. We've attempted to wash them in the rain, and we're trying to air them out. It's cold. We were told we'd need only one long-sleeved shirt and one pair of pants, so that's all I've brought and those are wet now too. The other runners, looking all beautiful and youthful, are out drinking and celebrating their muddy victories. I'm in a bad mood.

"Let's go all out and run as fast as we can tomorrow," I try to convince Ann. My pride can't take another day of moseying slowly along behind the others.

"You can go ahead," Ann says. "I don't mind bringing up the rear. I'll walk with George and the sweep."

"Well.... If you're sure you don't mind.... OK, then..."

Ann, despite her constant upbeat attitude, has a rare momentary breakdown.

157

"It's just that I can't believe I paid $2000 to run through cow poop!"

OK. It 's out on the table. She's having a terrible time because of the cow poop. I'm having a terrible time because...I can't stand having a terrible time in a race. I want to at least *try* to run. Finally, we're having a real conversation! I know Ann is unhappy at that moment and I feel guilty at having talked her into this trip. But as she sits there on her bed, dirty and frustrated and upset about the "cow poop," so different from her usual glamorous self, I feel the sudden urge to laugh. She looks better now, without makeup or clean pressed clothes, than I've ever seen her. Behind that perfect princessy exterior, she's opening up and admitting to having a shitty time! I don't hug her, because we're both gross Princesses at the moment, but I tell her what a good sport she is, and soon we are both smiling at the absurdity of vacationing in this muddy Mecca.

"It will get better," we tell each other.

October 14 9:00am

It's a sunny day! The terrain on this run is very similar to the Boulder foothills. Most of the crowd stayed up all night drinking. I feel proud as I run past that poor, young, guy with stomach cramps. I surprise myself by coming in with a great time – 15th place in this group of studs. Ann is not far behind me. She's happy with her time as well. We high-five each other. Princess Warriors rule!

October 14 11:00am

I'm standing at the top of a waterfall getting strapped into some kind of harness. I'm holding onto ropes and in a minute, I'm supposed to step off the edge of this cliff, and rappel my way down through that fall, to a pond below. The cliff is vertical. There's no climbing here. It looks like the idea is to make my legs horizontal and "walk" my way down the side of this cliff while I let out the slack in this rope. I'm panicked! I can't remember what the guide taught us in that 5 minute lesson. I was worrying about fainting while he was explaining it all. I'm a weakling! I know there are people around holding ropes, that I guess are somehow protecting me, but I have no idea how this all works. How can they be letting people like me, completely clueless airheads, climb down this cliff and through a waterfall?

Here I go! The water pummels my helmet! I look up. "DON'T LOOK UP!" the guide screams. OK. I get it now. That was a nice little demonstration about why we aren't supposed to look up. The pressure of the water on my eyes is liable to knock them out of their sockets. I'm hanging in the air, trying to position my feet against the side of the slippery vertical rocks. Slowly, I let out slack and move down. I'm getting the hang of it! Literally! Down I go, step by step, feeling like Indiana Jones! Yahoo! This is amazing!

Next is the zip-line to another section of the jungle. I soar through the air, hanging on to the cable with the special glove, tempted to let out a big Tarzan-style yell. (I was thinking it in my head, anyway. Despite the yoga training, I'm still shy about making guttural noises of any type.)

Devil: Yes, we know. It's another thing you really need to work on in the bedroom.

Angel: Dear, a simple purr usually works well, from what I hear. No need to imitate Tarzan.

We're surrounded by lush, tropical greenery. The trees have these gigantic leaves. It's as though we're in a movie set – Lilliputians wandering amongst these massive leaves and unnaturally green surroundings.

Three more waterfall descents, a walk across a wobbly suspension bridge, and three more zip line rides, and we reach the end of our guided adventure. With each scary event we'd been safely strapped to cables, but that didn't stop the adrenaline from filling my veins. This day is incredible! I'm beginning to understand what all this thrill-seeking fuss is about.

October 19 7am
On the airplane

What a week it's been. I flew into Costa Rica a nervous, Princess Worrier. I'm flying out a brave Princess Warrior. Well, I don't know if I really earned the title of "warrior." We didn't see any snakes and the adventure wasn't nearly as scary as I'd feared, but I faced the scary parts and survived. I only mildly freaked out when there was all

159

the horse play on the rafts. I think I only told ten people or so about the rafting accident of 2006 and Eileen's near-death experience. And I resisted yelling at the guide when even *he* was jumping up and down in the raft. Excuse me, but did he not know our lives were in danger?

I'm so glad Josh and Ann were here on this trip with me. There were other friends, too, but Josh, Ann, and I hung out together most of the time. We weren't into the late-night-parties that most of the others were, but we still enjoyed a glass of wine here and there or a quieter dinner soaking in the beautiful tropical scenery. After the cow-poop run, things did, indeed, get better. A lot better. The food, accommodations, and scenery were more than I could have ever hoped for. It ended up being a trip of a lifetime and I'm so glad I faced all my silly fears and didn't miss out on this experience.

I'd wondered all week if anything would happen between Josh and me. That first rainy night when I was cold, tired, and upset, Josh walked me to the door of my cabin. I thought he might give me a kiss, but he just gave me a hug goodnight.

His sweet innocence was charming. So different from the overtly suggestive Dick.

Angel: Here's someone that would keep you safe, Dear. I planted him right here to protect you!

Devil: You've been playing it safe your whole life, Sister. Haven't you learned anything?

The rest of the week Josh and I sat together at meals and on the bus. I'd throw out a flirtatious remark here and there. Josh would smile, but the unspoken words were there – "we're too different." Or possibly what he was thinking was "that's one nasty zit."

On the last night, when we were all out at a dance club, Josh, in his charming, shy way, showed me the ballroom dance steps he'd been learning from dance lessons back in Virginia. For a moment I wished I didn't have all the baggage of my past. If only I could be young again, that innocent girl that said her rosaries faithfully and believed in fairy tales and love. I wouldn't have an ex-husband, an FB, a Ryan, or an inner-Devil filling my mind with impure thoughts. I wish Josh could have known me then.

Funny that I'm sure I was too much of a prude for Dick and probably too risqué for Josh. I'm not sure what Josh thought of me. Whatever it was, it was pretty clear he wasn't interested in a romantic relationship. Since we live in different states and we *are* very different, I know it's just as well, but I can't help feeling sad. Even though it was only a week, Josh was my sweet protector on this trip. I managed everything just fine, but having him around gave me a sense of security and peace that I adored.

October 24

FB's little green dot shows up telling me he's online. We're both online a lot and IM'ing seems to be where we do most of our communicating. When he makes himself "invisible" it's as though he's shutting the door in my face – telling me he doesn't want to talk to me. He did this the whole time he was dating the Republican kissy-face girl. But then, one day, his green dot showed back up, and we started chatting daily again.

I've already told FB all about the trip, sent him pictures, filled him in on all the harrowing adventures. It's almost like we're regular friends. We talk a little about politics. Thanks to Saturday Night Live, everyone is talking about Sarah Palin. She does make the election more interesting. After a few minutes of idle chatter, I tell him that I'm going to a book club meeting close to where he lives.

yf> Should I stop by?
fb> Not tonight. I'm recovering.
yf> From what?
fb> burn
I'm immediately concerned.
yf> where?
fb> face
On his face! Oh no! He's been in an accident with his dirt bike.
yf>what happened??
fb>microderm procedure
yf> cosmetic?
fb> yes
yf> what a girl! Now I'm definitely coming over!
fb> why?
yf> to laugh at you!

FB looks ridiculous! I was hoping for this. I want to see him at his ugliest so that I'll stop being attracted to him. His face is all red and swollen, his eyelids puffy. He's wearing long johns, with one leg riding up. He looks like a big version of a little kid. It's obvious he's been sleeping when he answers the door. He lets me in and heads sleepily back up the stairs. I'm not sure what I'm supposed to do, but then he motions me to follow.

Sparky's happy to see me. A typical Golden Retriever, he's licking me and sticking his head in my crotch, begging me to pet him, as I'm sitting on FB's bed.

"Why did you do this?" I knew FB was always worried about his phat, but I never thought he worried about his phace!

"Wanted to get rid of some spots. Maybe it was a big mistake." He's plopped back down on the bed with his eyes closed, exhausted.

It's too bad he's so miserable. It means I can't even properly make fun of him. We talk for awhile and I ask him if there's anything he wants me to get for him. Then he pulls me down, to lay next to him on the bed. I resist and tell him I'm seeing someone now.

"Shhhh. Don't worry. I won't do anything," he whispers.

And he just holds me tightly like a security blanket.

Though I wish it weren't true, I find myself excited, even from this fully-clothed embrace. FB's in a lot of pain. He's vulnerable. He's lonely. He looks like a tomato. And right now he's getting comfort from holding me. I know how it is to be lonely and want something other than a pillow to hold at night.

I've been feeling very lonely and sad myself. Matt and Megan are living on their own now and don't need me anymore. And even Scotty is growing up. The night I got home from Costa Rica, I called Paul's to find out if Scotty could come home a day early. I was sure he'd want to. But both Paul and Scotty said, no – they were just sitting down to dinner and had plans for the evening. Scotty didn't even ask me about my trip or tell me he missed me! And no one seems to need me at work anymore, either. Everyone filled in for me while I was in Costa Rica, leaving me very little to do when I returned. Not a good thing when the company is facing layoffs.

Right now FB at least needs me and wants me to lay here with him. This feels so familiar and comfortable, almost like an old married

162

couple. I love to have his arms around me this way. I want him to depend on me...to at least love me as a friend, if not as a girlfriend.

Laying this close is having its effect on both of us. So much for just laying here as a comforting friend. There's some definite groping going on. I have to get out of here before I do something that I'll regret. Even though Ryan and I never agreed to exclusivity – in fact, I believe it was the opposite – he's been acting a lot like a boyfriend, and we did have that one night of sex, so it's not right for me to be here with FB. Besides, FB is in pain. I can't even kiss his face. And I really want to kiss more than his face. I get up and start collecting my things.

"Where are you going?"

"I can't do this. I'm in a relationship with someone now. And even if I weren't, I can't take it when you disappear."

"I don't disappear."

"Yes you do. And if you do it again, it will be the last time. If there's someone you want to date, or you think I'm getting too close, or you're really busy, just tell me. Don't disappear." I'm not saying this in an angry way, but I want to be firm.

"I won't disappear."

"Call me if you need anything." I tell him as I bend over him to kiss his shoulder goodbye.

I'm sick. Very sick. I'm here at the Best Buy Geek Squad Hospital, surrounded by other sick computers and laptops. I see them, many of them dying, their parts carelessly lying around. These geeks poke and prod. They run their diagnostics on me trying to figure out what's wrong with my performance. I'll tell you what's wrong! I'm old! And my cable's been tampered with! While Yvette's been running around in Costa Rica and tending to red-faced old boyfriends, I'm stuck here without power, fighting for my life.

November

November Goals

1. *Adventure: Something with Ian Usher?*
2. *Love: Ian Usher*
3. *Write: I'm Published! Submit another article for pay.*

Unbelievably, Ian Usher contacted me last month, asking if I was still interested in meeting up. He's the guy traveling around the world, trying to accomplish 100 goals in 100 weeks. In July, I'd emailed him telling him that I was planning to have an adventure a month, and that I wanted to try and meet him when he was in the US. It was really more of a "wouldn't that be cool if..." kind of email. I'd figured he'd have forgotten all about me by now, with all the people he's meeting and things he's doing. I read his blog and he's on the go constantly – a minor celebrity. If you google him, he's all over the news. But he did actually contact *me* and we've exchanged several emails at this point. I told him about my book and he said he'd be happy to be my Mr. November! I haven't yet told him that he's supposed to fall in love with me, too. One unrealistic thing at a time. First I have to figure out how to meet him. It would be a lot easier if I weren't freaked out about losing my job. I just took off a week last month, spending more than my vacation budget to go to Costa Rica and I'm flying out to LA to visit my sister, Michele, for Thanksgiving. Between parenting schedules, work and financial worries, I really can't afford either the time or money to go gallivanting around the country, chasing Ian Usher. But....wouldn't it be cool if....

A quick look at Ian's 100goals100weeks.com Website shows he's going to be at Grand Canyon, Vegas, and Mount Rushmore in mid-November. Those aren't totally out of the question. Maybe I can talk one of my friends into taking a road trip with me.

November 7 8am

It's a lot harder to give the "Let's Just Be Friends" speech after you've been dating awhile. Ryan and I only had sex that one time but that was enough for me to realize that sex without love just doesn't do it for me. I kept hoping my interest would grow, but it seems we have less and less to talk about. He calls me. I talk about something insignificant. He says "uh huh." I ask him what's going on with him. He says, "Not much."

Tonight he's coming to my house for dinner. I am going to have to talk to him about this, as difficult as it will be. I've written it down on my To Do List to keep myself from chickening out.

November 7 7pm

"Ryan, I don't think we're really connecting."

"You don't? I thought we were doing really well."

"Um, no. I wasn't really feeling that. We live so far apart, so it's difficult to really get to know each other. Our conversations are just small talk. We never talk about anything deep or personal. And we both are busy. I think we should explore other relationships."

"Are you breaking up with me?" Ryan says this in a hurt, surprised voice. I'm surprised he's surprised. I almost thought he'd be relieved.

"Well... I don't think I'd call it *breaking up*, since I never thought we were an established *couple*."

"You didn't think we were a couple? I haven't been dating anyone else. Have you?"

"Um, well, you know I went on that hike with Dick. And you knew I was meeting Josh in Costa Rica. And you're still going to Hawaii next month with Julie, so...we're both seeing other people, even if it is platonic. I don't think we've been acting much like a couple." I don't mention the fully-clothed grope session with FB.

"But we can still go out?" he asks.

"I guess so. I don't think we should have sex, though. And we should be free to explore other options."

"So, like, we can still kiss?"

"Yeah, I guess that would be OK." I'm a little uneasy about this. Kissing is nice, but if there's no future, I'm not sure if it's a great idea. But, hey, Ryan's a good kisser and I really don't want to hurt his feelings. We start cleaning up the dishes and go watch the two DVDs he's brought: a yoga movie and an episode from *Californication*.

November 7 10pm

"Can I ask you a personal question?" Ryan asks, mid-smooch.

166

"Of course! Anything."

Maybe Ryan's ready to initiate a meaningful conversation that has nothing to do with his cats.

"Have you ever thought about shaving the hair above your lips?"

This confuses me.

"Are you talking about....<long pause> ... pubic hair?" I ask in an unsure voice. Even though we are both fully clothed, we'd watched an episode of *Californication* less than an hour ago in which a sexy woman was talking about her "lips" – not the ones on her face. And, not that Ryan knows this, but I had recently been experimental in this regard, wondering if I'd gotten my recent attempt at a "landing strip" pubic hairstyle right. Being a complete novice, I was pretty sure it was a botched job, but I'm not planning on entering any vaginal beauty contests, so hadn't really been concerned.

Ryan laughs, indicating he was not talking about pubic hair. "No, I mean on your face."

"My face?" Now I'm even more confused. I can't believe he asked me this. He thinks I have a *mustache*? "No! I can honestly say I have never thought about shaving the hair above my lips! That's probably the only hair on my body that I've never worried about." *Until now!* "I didn't even think the hair on my face was visible. Can you see it?"

"Well, I can feel it when I kiss you," Ryan tells me.

Can you now? Well, this breaking up stuff just got a whole lot easier. I'm no longer the slightest bit concerned about hurting Ryan's feelings.

"Then I guess you shouldn't kiss me!"

"Julie says you can easily get rid of it."

I wish I could easily get rid of Julie.

"I have really sensitive skin. I don't want to start messing with shaving or waxing, because then it may get all red, and the hair will grow in coarse, and then it *will* look like I have a mustache!"

"Julie says that's just a myth. All women get rid of the hair there."

I try not to act upset. Even though I've never met her I'm sure Julie must have told this to Ryan when he caught her in the bathroom with shaving cream on her face and a Bic razor in hand. Maybe she's really a man. And Ryan? He doesn't have a clue what women go through trying to look good. Who does he think he is? Mary Kay? Maybe I'll get the razor and start shaving his nipples. I'll tell him Laptop Guy says that all men like their nipples cut off.

Ryan has the nerve to start kissing me again.

"Um... I really don't want to kiss you anymore, now that you told me you can feel my facial hair." I'm completely paranoid. I wonder if every person that's ever kissed me has felt the hair above my lip and thought I was a terrible bushy-lipped kisser.

Ryan tries to assure me that *it's OK*. He doesn't mind. *Well, sorry, Bucko, but our kissing days are over.*

As soon as Ryan leaves I examine my face carefully in the mirror. Those hairs are tiny. I never even noticed them. I run my tongue along my upper lip trying to simulate what it must feel like to kiss me. I also try bringing my lower lip up to the offending area between my upper lip and nose, but I can't feel anything. While I'm examining my face at different angles, I point my nostrils into the mirror, and take a gander up my nose. Not a pretty site. Thank goodness no one sticks their tongue in *there*. Great! Now I'm going to be insecure about kissing. As if I'm not already insecure enough about everything else.

November 8

Ryan calls and suggests we go to Glenwood Springs at the end of December. He knows of a place that is decorated beautifully for the holidays. I guess he forgot that last night he told me I had a mustache.

"Didn't we decide to be just friends last night?" I ask him.

"We can go as friends." He assures me.

I'm amused by this. "Do you only go on weekend getaways with girlfriends that are just friends?" I don't want to take Julie's place as the "interfering platonic girlfriend."

"No. It's just that I never had a chance to go out of town with you. And everything is all lit up and looks beautiful and romantic over the holidays." Ryan tells me.

I don't want to go to Glenwood Springs with Ryan. I don't want to see Ryan any more. Any thought of Ryan reminds me of that humiliating conversation about my hairy lip.

"Maybe," I tell him. "I'm going to be pretty busy in December with the holidays."

Devil: Maybe? Why are you still talking to this guy? You should be asking him if he's ever thought about shaving his hairy ass.

Angel: Really, Dear. I know you're trying to be nice, but it would really be better to be honest and tell him you've decided to become a nun. Then you will never have to worry about any kind of hair.

I know I should have just told him I didn't want to see him any more, but I still feel guilty that I had sex with him when I wasn't really that interested in him. I've always at least stayed friends with guys I've gone out with before, but I just feel ashamed and embarrassed about my relationship with Ryan. I guess I'm getting what I deserve. Not only will I never have sex, I probably will never even kiss anyone again.

November 9

None of my friends want to take a road trip with me to join Ian Usher on any of his adventures and I don't want to go alone. It's just as well. I'm tired and depressed and lonely. I'm in no mood for dating or romance or even adventures. I'll find something to do with my sister, Michele, when I visit her in California for Thanksgiving, and that will be my adventure.

November 11

FB's green dot has disappeared again. I call him up.

"I told you that if you disappeared, I'd get mad."

"What are you talking about?"

"You made yourself invisible on IM. Why did you do that? It makes me feel like you're avoiding me."

"I'm not avoiding you. Other people chat with me, too, and sometimes I'm just not in the mood for chatting. It's not all about you, ya know." FB is chuckling as he's saying this. Maybe I am just being sensitive.

"That's about the only way you ever communicate with me, so don't make yourself invisible. Or at least tell me why you're making yourself invisible. Are you seeing someone?"

"No. I'll change it right now. There. I'm visible again. Do you want to send me an IM?"

"Well, I do want to ask you something."

"Ask away."

"Do you think I have a mustache?"

"What are you talking about?"

"That guy I was going out with. I broke up with him the other night and he told me he could feel the hair on my upper lip when he kissed me." I'm hoping that FB will reassure me that I'm a good kisser and he never noticed any hair on my upper lip. Or maybe he'll suggest I should come over and he'd test it out and let me know. Instead he says, "Since I have a mustache, I wouldn't know, but if you want to get rid of it, I can give you the name of someone." Figures. I'd forgotten FB has experience with cosmetic procedures.

"I just wanted to know if you ever noticed it."

"Nope. I did notice that hair on your chin, though."

"Very funny."

This conversation doesn't make me feel any better about my face. I feel slightly reassured that FB's not pulling his disappearing act again, though I'd been hoping that once he'd heard I was free, there would be at least a hint of interest. He may not be purposely avoiding me, but something's going on with him.

November 13

I'm awake as usual, enjoying a very early morning romp with Laptop Guy. Ian's blog post this morning was about fulfilling his 14th goal: Visiting the Grand Canyon. I'm always interested in Ian's blog. His photos and descriptions of all he's seeing are exciting and entertaining. But today's entry was the first I've read where he admitted to feeling a bit lonely. The last paragraphs read:

I eventually drove along to the Grand Canyon Visitor Centre, and found a place at the campsite to park up, and caught the free shuttle bus back to the canyon rim to watch the sun set. It was lovely to see, but I felt pretty much alone, as this is the first goal that I have achieved without anyone coming along to join me. And as the canyon walls became tinged with orange, I became slightly tinged with melancholy. It would be nice to share this with someone.

I was reminded very much of the words of Christopher McCandless in the movie "Into the Wild", when he realized:-
"Happiness is only real when shared."

170

Ian's words reminded me of a blog post I had written myself, called, "Single But Not Alone," after I'd run the Disney World Marathon using my Virtual Running Buddy idea. My blog post from that time ended with:

I may have come to Orlando alone, but today I felt less alone than I ever felt when I was married. Maybe the key to not being alone is to let people in your life. I don't think I did enough of that when I was married. I'm learning that being single isn't about being alone. Being single may have helped me learn to be less lonely than I've ever been in my life.

My own words help push me out of the funk I've been in. I wish I had made the effort to get out to the Grand Canyon to share that with Ian. I'd really wanted to. But in the end, I was too afraid to go alone. November isn't over yet. Maybe there's still a possibility I can meet him. I send him an email to explore the idea.

From: yvette.francino@gmail.com
To: ian@100goals100weeks.com
Thu, Nov. 13 4:26am

Hi Ian,

I think this journey of yours is incredible, but I so understand that melancholy feeling you described in your last blog post. I'd wanted to join you for the Grand Canyon, but I couldn't get away...parenting and work schedules do get in the way sometimes! I am going to be in LA visiting my sister's family for Thanksgiving week...Nov.24-28. Your calendar isn't specific about exactly where you'll be that week, but if it happens to find you in Southern California, then maybe I will get that November meeting in after all.

Oh...by the way, I accomplished one of my goals this month....I got published in a real magazine....Colorado Runner! I wrote an article about my Virtual Running Buddy experience. Yippee! The book is

next! Always remember that you are inspiring many of us to follow our dreams!

Happy Travels,
Yvette

Hi there,
Congratulations on getting into print! Well done you! Big virtual pat on the back! (VPB)

Well, well, well. Looks like I might yet make it as Mr November. I am currently in Las Vegas, and fly to Rapid City this weekend. Back to Las Vegas on Monday, a couple more days here, then off to LA. I reckon I will arrive perhaps 20th, and may be down in San Diego 21st to 23rd. Then in LA 24th to 30th!!!!!!

So, let's make it happen!

Ian

November 15

Wow. I never thought I'd actually meet Ian and now that it looks like I'm going to, I have to figure out what we're going to do. After some quick internet searching to find a cheap November "adventure," I discover that audience viewing at the LA studios is offered for free. I quickly confer with Michele and we decide the most convenient date/time is a showing of "The Big Bang Theory!" in Warner Bros. Studio at 7:00 on November 25th. Ian is in. I invite Michele and her two daughters to join us. Back when I was in my fantasy world, I'd imagined Ian and I would fall in love. At the very least, I'd imagined a "real date" without a chaperone. But I'm so tired of the whole dating scene and still haven't recovered from the "mustache incident" with Ryan. Ian is probably confused by my intentions as well. I had initially implied I wanted a date and now I'm changing it to a family outing. It will probably be a relief for him.

November 25 2pm

The doorbell to Michele's West Hills house rings at 2pm. Ian had asked if I might want to accompany him on a ride up Mulholland

172

Drive to see the Hollywood sign on the hill. Michele and the girls are going to meet us at the studio. Since this was all Ian's suggestion I'm both flattered and nervous that this is feeling like a "date" again. However, once I start talking to Ian, I'm immediately at ease. He has this fantastic accent and a friendly personality. After a few minutes I feel as if we're old friends.

"Maggie, show us the way," Ian asked of his Magellan GPS. *Someone that talks to his GPS? Oh, I like this guy!*

We chat along the way, with Maggie only occasionally interrupting. Ian openly answers all my questions about his trip, his thoughts, and even the breakup of his marriage. His condition is only that I do the same and so we exchange stories. He has an easy going nature and has this habit of saying "I reckon this" or "I reckon that" which mixed with his accent makes him sound a bit like an English cowboy.

This detour out to the LA area wasn't on Ian's original itinerary. I find out that earlier in the day, Ian sold the rights to his Life4Sale story to Disney films. He really is going to be famous!

"So, who's going to play you in your movie? Hugh Grant?" I ask.

"I suggested George Clooney," he answers, "and the agent took me quite seriously and told me she'd look into it!" he answers with that wonderful accent.

"You sound much more like Hugh Grant," I tell him.

"Yes, but he's got funny hair, don't ya think? And who would you like to play you? I've already gotten a couple of requests for Julia Roberts so you'll have to pick someone else."

"That's fine. I'll take Meg Ryan." Julia Roberts laughs too loudly.

"Right-o."

We stop at every overlook, though most are not worth stopping for. The weather is gloomy and the scenery, really very disappointing, but I'm enjoying every minute. Ian asks me to help navigate. (He hasn't yet learned that I'm navigationally challenged.) He has a detailed map on his HP computer (which I name, "Harry Potter".) I tell Ian (and Harry Potter) about Laptop Guy. Ian says that he doubts his laptop is a male, and he really only likes to talk to Maggie because she has a voice. Poor Harry (or Harriet) Potter. I

173

assure HP that Ian really loves him (or her) despite the lack of obvious gender.

When Ian is taking pictures, I make a quick call to Michele to let her know that all is well, and in fact, I'm having a wonderful time! She says she has a headache and asks if it would be OK if she and the girls skip meeting us at the studio. I refrain from acting too excited (Michele does have a headache, after all – I don't want to yell out "Yippee!") but I do tell her it's perfectly fine.

Ian and I continue our drive. "Have you ever had any mishaps as you've been traveling?" I ask him.

"I reckon we should find some wood to knock on, but, no, everything has gone amazingly to plan."

We continue following the meandering road towards the famous HOLLYWOOD letters on the hill, and then, as the excitement builds, we run into a gate. Signs warn us the road is closed.

"Just four-wheel it," I advise. "Let's have a real adventure."

"That sounds like a great idea since this isn't my car," Ian jokes. Instead, he tries a different route, and when that doesn't work, he tries yet a third route. In the end we give up, Ian telling me that this is his first ever foiled adventure.

"No worries," I assure him. "The real adventure is being in the live studio audience at The Big Bang Theory!" I remind him. "A unique, free LA experience!"

November 25 6:30 pm

After a quick bite at Pepper Thai, we head to the studio. My only duty was to deliver the proper address, and I mistakenly give the wrong one. We only waste 10 or 15 minutes with that detour until we find our proper destination.

We soon learn that this plan is a bust as well. No wonder it was so easy to get these tickets. There are like thousands of people that have also gotten free tickets – many more tickets than there are seats. We take our place at the end of the "queue," as Ian calls it. Perhaps if we had been here earlier, we might have gotten a spot, but there are a lot of people ahead of us who suffer the same fate.

I'm kind of bummed that I didn't research the whole studio audience thing better, but Ian is not discouraged. "What about the Santa Monica Pier?" he asks.

"Sure!" I love that Ian is able to roll with the punches and wants to share my November adventure with me. We see the famous Ferris wheel from a distance, looking beautiful with the colorful changing lights. "What a great idea!" I love the thought of riding the beautiful Ferris wheel with Ian – romantic and high above the LA lights. Perfect! Much better than watching a sitcom in a studio audience.

It's lightly raining, but that doesn't stop us. We make our way to the park and gaze at the Ferris wheel, looking like a fireworks display with it's colorful designs. As we get closer, however, we find that, despite the lights, the amusement park is closed. I guess it doesn't operate on rainy nights in November.

This is so disappointing. I must have an adventure! The month is almost over!

I suddenly get an idea as I look out over the Pacific.

"Ya know... I've never been skinny dipping before."

Ian looks at me skeptically. "You realize that ocean is really cold right now."

"Let's just go dip our toes in," I tell him. "Then I'll decide."

We walk down, pull our shoes and socks off, roll up our pants, and step into the shallow water, letting our feet sink down in the sand. It's cold, but not frigid. I was planning on making The Polar Plunge last March. Surely I can do this.

"I'm gonna do it." I declare.

"You're sure? It IS awfully cold out there. And there are a few people around."

Now I am getting cold feet, and not just because of the water temperature. "You'd have to look the other way." I tell Ian. "And I'm not sure what I'd do about towels. I also don't want to get my hair all wet. I might get the seat of your car all wet. But I have to do something for the November adventure."

I'm going back and forth, in my usual indecisive way, talking about the pros and cons, when suddenly Ian starts stripping down. "If you're going to do this," he says in that very cool accent, "I reckon you best get on with it." And before I know it, he's in the ocean, diving through the waves like a dolphin! "Come on in!" he yells.

175

I can't chicken out now. I hurry out of my clothes, run in a little more than waist-deep. Yikes! It *is* freezing! It's the most wonderful, freezing, ocean I've ever stepped foot in. Me. The girl who feels embarrassed to look at herself nude in a mirror, is skinny dipping. And with my newfound lack of inhibition I let out a very loud, "Woo Hoo!!"

November 25 10:30 pm

Wet and slightly shivering in our jeans and sweaters, Ian insists on finding a place to celebrate my bravery. We call Michele and she suggests Geoffrey's. My, this is a posh place. This is where the Beverly Hills elite probably come to have a drink. I don't think anyone else in this place recently went skinny dipping. What prudes! We order our very expensive drinks and clink our glasses. "To the best adventure ever!"

I ask Ian if there are any red flags he worries about when dating. Someone with kids? Someone with baggage? Someone that's older? No, he doesn't say any of those things. "I guess I'd consider it a red flag if the girl has a mustache." *A mustache!* I don't hear anything about mustaches my entire life, and now twice in a month!

I tell the Ian the story of my break up with Ryan. He assures me, whilst laughing at the embarrassing story, that I don't have a mustache – he had been making a joke by picking some outlandish red flag. I squelch the urge to check the mirror for the millionth time to ensure the tiny hairs on my upper lip haven't grown.

Ian says he asks everyone that joins him for his goals the same question: "What is your motivation? Why did you want to meet and join me?"

"Because I admire what you're doing," I answer honestly. "Traveling around the world, meeting all these people, living out your dreams – it's something most of us don't have the courage to do." Then I added, "And, of course, you're cute."

"So is a kiss included in this November Adventure?"

"I hope so."

Ian leans over and gives me a kiss.

"Did you feel my mustache?" I ask him.

"Wait. Let me test it again to be sure." Another kiss. "Nope, not a bit."

Ian's cooking me dinner in his RV – spaghetti with marinara sauce made with specialty ground lamb meat and homemade port. Both of these delicacies were given to Ian during his travels by one of the many generous people he has met during this whirlwind tour of the world. Two nights in a row with the same guy. A guy that I really like! This is all cozy, just like he's my boyfriend except that after tonight I'll probably never see him again. I'd hoped Michele would ask him to join us for Thanksgiving dinner. Ian has plans with a juggler tomorrow, but he offered to make me dinner tonight, and I'm thoroughly enjoying myself.

Ian's stories are fascinating.

"What's the most generous thing you've been given on this trip?" I ask him.

He thinks awhile. "That's a good question. I've been given a lot of gifts." He tells me of all the people that have offered him places to stay, things to eat, special souvenirs, a beautiful painting. "The one that may have been the most personal was from the guy that cleaned up my tattoo. He was a big, burly guy. The type of guy a lot of people might be scared of because of his size and his tattoos." Ian went on to tell me the story of the gift that had been given to him by the tattoo artist.

"Many years ago, he'd lost a significant person from his life and had felt like his life had no direction. An older Indian woman from the Pine Ridge Indian Reservation listened to his story and gave him a peculiar ring. Instead of a stone there was a maze engraved on the front of the ring. She told him the ring symbolized finding his path in life. He went on to build his business, get married and have four children. After talking to his wife about it, he decided to give me the ring. Some day, when it's the right time, I'll pass it on to someone else." Ian shows me the ring that he's wearing – gold with the labyrinth design. The story is beautiful and moves me. I feel like I'm also searching my way through a labyrinth, wondering when I will be out. The end is in sight, I know. Just around a corner. (I don't tell Ian this, because I don't want him to think I'm hinting for him to give me the ring. After all, he just got it!)

I suddenly feel guilty that I haven't given Ian anything. Instead of giving, I'm taking! He's the one that helped me accomplish one of my goals. I didn't help him accomplish anything. I'm here eating the food that other people have given him instead of giving him anything myself.

Ian tells me more stories, showing me the accompanying photos or videos. He has so much to tell. 100 goals in 100 weeks – and these are big goals! I think of my little adventures – so insignificant in comparison. I'd been so proud of the skinny-dipping escapade – probably the most daring thing I'd done all year – and I didn't even get my hair wet!

November 26 10pm

Finally, I'm here with someone I'm very attracted to. He's funny, intelligent, and good-looking. Ian is a classic Enneagram Type 7:

> *Sevens are enthusiastic about almost everything that catches their attention. They approach life with curiosity, optimism, and a sense of adventure, like "kids in a candy store" who look at the world in wide-eyed, rapt anticipation of all the good things they are about to experience. They are bold and vivacious, pursuing what they want in life with a cheerful determination.*

I don't think I've ever met anyone that more meets this description than Ian. His willingness to try anything new is refreshing. And here he is with me. A perfectly willing Mr. November! Jeannine had described me as being "enthralled" with Ian. I don't know if I'd exactly use that word because it makes me sound like a mindless groupie, but it's true that I've been kind of cyberstalking this guy and I am completely fascinated with his story. And here we are, making out in his RV.

Devil: Do you think maybe we could have a climax in this book?

Angel: He sounds like an interesting man, Dear. Let's hope he doesn't ask you anything about your body hair like that last unfortunate gentleman.

Sex or no sex? That is the question. I wish the Angel hadn't brought up Ryan. I remember the regrettable discovery that sex without love was very disappointing. I almost convince myself that this is different. I could love Ian. Then I look at all these pictures of the places Ian is seeing, the experiences he's having, and the people he's doing them with. Some of them are young, hot, sexy people. Do I really want to sleep with a guy that has the opportunity for 100 girls in 100 weeks? Not that I think Ian is that kind of guy. At the end of 100 weeks, he'd probably only sleep with 50 girls – 75 max.

But why should I worry about those women (outside of my fear of catching an STD)? Why can't I just live in the moment, the way Ian does? Wouldn't it be nice to just enjoy this night without thoughts of the past or the future? Ian wonders the same thing. Why not?

"Because, we're not in love. It might be great tonight, but I'll read your blog and follow your journey and realize that you are meeting lots of women. And I'll feel lonely and sad. If it had been the beginning of the year, I'd so take advantage of this situation. But now I know better. The next time I have sex, I want it to be special. I don't want to just have a one night stand."

Ian doesn't argue or try to persuade me that it would be any different. He's not going to make me any false promises – another thing I respect about him.

"OK, then. I reckon I should get you back to your sister's, eh?"

"I guess so," I say reluctantly.

As we drive back to Michele's house, we talk more about Ian's 100 goals and his future plans. I really wish I had helped him with one of his goals or at least experienced one with him.

"What are the most daring goals on your list?" I ask.

"Well, there are the ones the media makes a big deal about. Running with the bulls, driving a car into water off a jetty, and, of course, The Mile High Club."

"I'm in the Mile High Club!"

"You've had sex in an airplane?"

"Well, no. But I've had sex in Denver, and that is the Mile High City."

"Doesn't count." says Ian.

"Well. I could help you get in the Mile High Club."

"Really? I thought you wanted to be in love!"

"If it helps you make one of your goals, I'll make a sacrifice. Maybe we won't be in love, but it certainly will be an experience we're apt to remember, it will be special, and it will undoubtedly move me out of my comfort zone. It's got all the makings for a great finale for my book. Do you think we could schedule this for December?"

Ian's plans for December include driving up the West coast, and eventually ending in Alaska where he'll be dog sledding – nothing that really gives opportunity for a quick entry to the Mile High Club. So it doesn't look like this is going to happen, at least not in time for my book climax.

Devil: As if you'd do it anyway.
Angel: An airplane lavatory is quite difficult to maneuver, Dear. I don't think you'd really find it special.

Ian tells me he'll be in Colorado next summer, achieving his 7 Peaks in 7 Days goal. He also has Whitewater Rafting on his list, and by now, I'm an expert at that. Whether it's in a raft, at the top of a mountain, or in an airplane bathroom, I have no doubt that I'll see Ian again.

We get to Michele's . I wish Ian luck, telling him how wonderful it has been to have met him. For the last two evenings I've been enamored with his amazing adventures, his optimistic attitude, and his uncanny ability to experience so much life each day. And for this moment, I have no worries about the past or the future or even the hair above my lip, but simply close my eyes and thoroughly enjoy our kiss goodbye.

November 27 Thanksgiving

Ah, life is good. I'm lying here on this pillow-plumped chaise with Laptop Guy, while Michele is in the kitchen preparing yummy-smelling Thanksgiving dishes. The last two nights when I've returned to Michele's home from my outings with Mr. November, the guest room has been adorned with roses Michele had picked from her garden, a lit scented candle, and even chocolate mints on the pillow! I've been loving this! Bed & Breakfasts are my favorite types of establishments, and Chez Michele's has now become my favorite.

What makes this pseudo B&B more special than any other isn't the candles or the food. Yesterday, I got a lazy late morning invitation from my brother-in-law, Ray, to go on a long run in the 70-degree perfect California weather. Usually a reticent fellow, we chatted the whole way, discussing religion, politics, and even relationships! The cat drapes herself around me. The two golden retrievers beg to be petted, their chins in my lap, looking up at me with their puppy-dog eyes. I get random hugs of affection from my nieces, nephew, and sister, not because I'm saying 'hello' or 'goodbye' – just because they love me. B&B's usually don't come stocked with people who give you a quick hug and kiss as you walk by.

I, of course, revel in all the attention. On other Thanksgivings I've been busy with my own preparations, either cooking or parenting or at least helping the hostess. This time Michele insists on fully spoiling me and I have to do nothing but lounge around and be served. And – get this – she actually seems to be enjoying doing all this pampering! Yesterday, she didn't even complain when I shouted up to the "front desk" (also known as the kitchen) for someone to bring me shampoo. Instead she brought me an assortment of toiletries including the requested shampoo, hair conditioner, powder, hand cream and mouthwash! They were all unopened in their cute mini containers, just waiting for the perfect guest with dirty hair, dry skin, and bad breath. This place is like magic! *Quick, what else can I ask for? I know if I yell over for love, the dogs will come bounding in along with the rest of the family, but I need some time to check email.*

And what a surprise I get. I have an email from Megan with the subject line: "READ THIS IMMEDIATELY AND CALL ME!" My heart starts beating faster and my stomach flips. What could this be? Has some sort of emergency happened while I've been off running around in LA, putting my family on hold?

It's a photo of a pregnancy test. "Two lines means positive!" she writes with an arrow to the double-lined test. Oh my God! I take a silent moment to let it sink in – my stomach does flip flops at the news. Tears well up in my eyes. A baby. There is nothing more miraculous than a baby.

"Woo Hoo!" I yell out to whoever can hear me at Chez Michele's. (I've become better about yelling out loud, rather than simply in my head.)

"I'M GOING TO BE A GRANDMA!"

Things I'm thankful for:
- My new power cable, free from kinks.
- The electricity soaring into me, filling me with renewed strength.
- Yvette is no longer going out with that Laptop-murdering low life human, Ryan.
- Yvette didn't fall in love with that androgynous Laptop Chap, HP.
- My Device Family: Blackberry, iPod, Desktop Guy, and Tom-Tom.

December

December Goals
1.   *Adventure: ????*
2.   *Love: ????*
3.   *Write: ????*

This is it. The final month in 2008. I have no idea what my adventure is going to be. I don't feel like having an adventure. I'm tired. And it doesn't look like I'm going to fall in love, either. And if I don't fall in love, I might as well forget about this whole book idea. According to *"How to Get a Book Published,"* books in the romance genre must end with the man and woman falling in love and living happily ever after. I wouldn't exactly classify this book as a romance, but still... what kind of story will this be if I don't fall in love? It will just be a depressing diary of a desperate middle-aged woman. I set out at the beginning of the year determined to find a systematic approach to falling in love and all I've done is show that I can't do it. I haven't discovered any magic formula. I feel like such a failure.

Sure, all those fiction writers can wrap up their books with a nice, neat ending where things all fall into place. It's not so easy when you're writing a memoir! Except in *Eat, Pray, Love.* Even in that memoir, Elizabeth Gilbert conveniently falls in love at the end. Would it have been a best seller if she hadn't fallen in love? I think not! Who would even buy a book that was just called, *Eat, Pray*? You've gotta have love or it's just not a good story!

OK. Enough of this. I must have a positive attitude! I still have 31 days. It might happen. If it gets to be December 31 and I still haven't figured out my adventure or fallen in love, I will kiss a stranger at midnight. That's pretty adventuresome, right? Undoubtedly the stranger will be "the one." My love goal fulfilled right in the nick of time. Maybe it will even allow for the sequel, which will be about my relationship with this mystery man.

183

December 5

I'm exhausted. I've been taking Ambien for insomnia and Lexapro for depression for 2 months. This, like the upper-lip-hair removal recommendation, came to me from Ryan and, indirectly, from his friend, Julie. These people should never practice medicine. I'm not noticing any improvements to my moods or energy. If anything, they seem to be getting worse. I tell the doctor about other weird symptoms. I've been dizzy, light-headed, unable to focus.

The doctor gives me a complete exam and sends me on my way to the lab to get blood work and to radiology for my annual mammogram.

There are a lot of drama queens out there that will tell you mammograms are "horrible." They'll tell you war stories about how their friend was in the "squished" position when the power went out and she had to stand there "for hours" in unbearable pain. Some even have the nerve to compare this experience with childbirth.

Clearly these women that scare mammogram-virgins with their stories are not comfortable with experimentation and sexual openness. For those of us that are single and don't have access to men who regularly fondle our breasts, the annual mammogram can provide a sexual adventure like none other.

Today's the day. No deodorant allowed. It's OK. Mr. Roboto and I enjoy our natural scents. I wear the hospital gown parted down the middle, just hinting of the breasts beneath. I open the gown slowly and the technician gently cups my breast, placing it gingerly on the tray as the robot enjoys this bit of foreplay. He, of course, is immediately turned on and starts coming down on me.

"Hold your breath so I can get a good picture" the technician advises. I do as told, keeping quiet, squelching my urges to moan. I whisper a quiet "oooh...that hurts so good" under my breath once the arm starts lifting. *Domo Arigato, Mr. Roboto*. We get into several different positions, doing "it" at different angles, the photographer guiding us through every shot. I work the camera, knowing my breasts are being handled by a professional.

The session is over too soon. The technician goes out to check the proofs while I have a quiet moment with Mr. Roboto. Still flustered from our sexy photo shoot, I'm tempted to disrobe entirely and wrap myself around his steely pole. But I feel chilly and somehow, the

184

machine seems distant. It's funny how one moment he can be squeezing my breasts...the next he's just sitting there, uncommunicative and cold. I have a moment of melancholy. I'm just another pair of breasts to him. He'll feel thousands before he touches mine again.

"Would you like to be my Mr. December?" I ask him. He sits there, saying nothing and I wonder if he cares about me at all. Machines....

The technician comes back and tells me the photos are good and I'm free to go.

Even though the robot is immobile, I know he is a complex being. It's not his fault that he has no life. It's not like he can run off to see the wizard like the Tin Man.

Even if I mean nothing to him, I will savor the sweet experience of our yearly rendezvous. He may not love me, but I know he's looking out for me and some day, may even save my life. Each relationship is different and we have to love it for what it is.

Goodbye you hunky robot. I'll see you next year.

December 7

Christmas Tree Cutting Day! This year it's just Megan, Scotty, Michael, and me. Matt, my older son, is trekking in Nepal and all of Michael's kids have other things going on. This is the fourth year Michael has helped us with this tradition. The first time, in 2005, was during that brief period that Michael and I had actually dated. FB and I had broken up (for the first time) and I'd told the kids that I didn't think I could handle cutting down a big tree and hauling it down the mountain. Megan asked if I could find someone on *Match.com* that owned a truck. I'd only been on one date with Michael, but I'd asked if he had a truck and told him about my dilemma. He said, as a matter of fact, he did have a truck and he agreed to help us with our Christmas Tree.

This is the first year Michael's daughter, Morgan, isn't joining us. She's a popular teen and busy with teen-stuff. But, luckily, Michael is still up for the trip. It's a good thing. There's no way we'd be able to do this without him. Every year I think I should put my foot down with the kids and insist we get a smaller tree. But Scotty loves having huge trees that rise 20 feet, taking advantage of the vaulted ceiling in the corner of our family room.

We scour the designated areas looking for a tree that will suffice, but none of them are satisfactory. Most are scrawny. Some look decent from afar, but when you get closer you see they are clumped and it is really two or three trees so close together that they look like one. Finally, Scotty finds one that he likes. It's gigantic. And it's in the wooded area – not really the "Christmas Tree" area. We look through the permit material and can't find anything that says we can't cut it down. I look at Michael questioningly. He looks back at me kind of with an "Are you sure you want to do this?" and we both see that Scotty is very sure that *this is the tree.* So Michael gets out the axe and starts chopping.

This isn't an easy tree to chop down and Michael is working hard. The ranger comes by and reprimands us for cutting a tree down outside of the permitted area, but he lets us get by without a fine. The tree finally comes down. Though Megan, Scotty, and I are not much help, we drag the tree and get it secured on the top of Michael's relatively new Expedition (he's upgraded from a truck.) I pray that the thing won't damage the SUV and will stay secure as we drive home.

When we get home, Michael is put to work again, helping to drag that heavy tree into the family room and into its stand. It looks pretty in the traditional place in the corner of the family room. Michael hasn't complained at all, despite all the hard work we've required of him today. He knows I want my kids to have the same kind of Christmas they've always had, complete with big tree. I feel so grateful to him for helping me keep this tradition alive.

Since the kids weren't with me for Thanksgiving, we're celebrating today with turkey, stuffing, and the other fixings. Son-in-law, Chris is here, too, drinking beer and watching football with Michael while I'm making dinner. Listening to the cheering sounds from the other room is like the smell of coffee.

I'm sure you're wondering, "How is listening to football like the smell of coffee?" Let me explain. I don't drink coffee myself, but I love the smell. It's warm and comforting. I just breathe in the aromas and that comfort and warmth fills me. It reminds me of when I was married and woke up in the morning to that familiar smell. I'd taken it for granted. I didn't realize how I would miss it until it was no longer there.

And that's what I'm feeling as I'm listening to Chris and Michael watching football in the other room. It reminds me of the many Thanksgivings I've shared with family where the men get all excited about football and the women are filling the kitchen with delicious smells. I know that may be rather old fashioned and sexist, but it's true. I miss having a man in my home. It fills me up, like the smell of coffee. When it's just me here, the sole adult in this house, we don't drink coffee and we don't watch football. But today – I almost forget I'm single.

December 10

FB and I are out to lunch. Tai Gun is one of FB's favorite sushi places. I think it was the first place we went out to lunch, years ago. FB, hasn't exactly *disappeared*, but he's being much quieter than usual. Typical that now that I'm no longer dating anyone, FB is no longer sending me suggestive messages. I've invited him to sushi because my friend, Ravi, is in India this month and I need a lunch buddy. I have an ulterior motive as well.

"I need a Mr. December to finish out my book."

"Why don't you find someone from *Match.com*?"

"I'm done with that," I tell him. "My subscription runs out soon and I'm too picky. I don't want to meet anyone new." Of course, I'm hoping he'll suggest doing something with me, but he's not.

"Are *you* going out with anyone?" I ask.

"Nope." As usual, FB's keeping quiet about his own love life. I don't want him to feel pressured, but I do have this book to finish. It would be nice if he could at least consider the fact that I need a good ending. If he's not going out with anyone else, this would be the time to play the part of the hero and realize he loves me.

December 15

OK, I'm desperate. No more of this hinting around stuff. It's time to directly ask FB to come in and save the day. Scotty is going to be with his Dad from December 29th – January 2nd. I have no plans for New Year's Eve. I have no December Adventure planned. I have no Mr. December. I see FB's online.

187

yf>Hey There.
fb>Hey. How's it going?
yf>Good except I need a Mr. December. What are you doing New Year's Eve?
fb>Donna and I are going out.

This stings. Who the heck is Donna? And why is he saying her name as though they are some kind of established couple and I should know this person.

yf>Donna?
fb>Yes, we've been seeing each other for about a month.

I call FB up.

"You've been going out with someone for a month? Why didn't you tell me?"

"There wasn't a good time to tell you."

"How about last week when we were at lunch and I asked you?"

"Well, we were just chit-chatting then. Nothing was official."

So now it's *official?* What does that mean? Are they getting married? He's never acted like anything was official before. Even when he was *officially* my boyfriend, he never really acted like anything was *official.* I had thought he just wasn't capable of being in a serious relationship at all. But it was just me. He didn't want to be in a serious relationship with *me.*

"You sound like you're serious."

"Yes. I really think this could be the real deal."

I know I should be happy for FB, but I'm not. He's not the one that's spent an entire year looking for someone to fall in love with. He's not the one needing a totally unrealistic but romantic ending for a book. Why does he get to fall in love? This isn't fair. This is not supposed to be what happens.

All year when "bad" stuff happened, like that stupid scene when Ryan asked me if I ever thought about shaving above my lips, it was embarrassing, yes; but in the back of my mind I'd think, "This will make a good scene for my book!" It kind of helped take the hurt out of the negative stuff. It made for good drama or at least a funny story.

But, in this case, I don't care enough about my book to think to myself it makes a good story. We're at the end of this book. This is when the good stuff is supposed to happen. If I don't fall in love with someone, the book will be more pathetic than ever. And with only two weeks to go, it's not going to happen.

I really don't want to cry, especially not while I'm on the phone with FB.

"You should have told me. You said you were my friend and a friend would have told me last week when I asked. You could have at least told me there was someone, even if it wasn't *official*." I know I'm being unreasonable. I'm mad at him and I have no right to be. We haven't been in a committed relationship for years. He doesn't need to tell me anything.

"I'm sorry," he says.

"I can't do this anymore. I thought it would be OK if I loved you, even if you didn't love me, because how can it ever be bad to love someone? Your parents are both dead and I thought you would need someone like me who would love you unconditionally. I thought I'd be OK if we were friends. That we'd be happy for each other if we found someone else. But I'm not happy that you found someone and I didn't. And you don't need my love. I know you'll never love me and it's just awkward when someone loves you if you don't feel the same way. So...I need to let you go." I'm crying now after all. A lot.

FB doesn't know what to say. "Let's just wipe the slate clean. I know you're upset now, but I'll be a better friend. I promise."

"I can't be your friend. If you ever decide you love me, let me know. Otherwise, I need you to let me go, too."

We say goodbye, probably for the last time. The end of the relationship at last.

It crosses my mind that maybe by New Year's Eve, he'll break up with *Donna,* and call me, declaring his love. That's what would happen in a fictional story. In *When Harry Met Sally*, Harry finds Sally at the New Year's Party, finally realizing he's in love.

December 16 8am

When I call the doctor to tell her I'd experienced double-vision when driving, she wants me to come in immediately for an MRI. Yippee! VIP-treatment! Mental note: When seeking quick medical attention, you are taken much more seriously when you complain about double vision, than when you complain about mood swings. The double vision this morning was a weird experience – one I can barely remember, to be perfectly honest. I'd dropped Scotty off at school, and

189

vaguely remember seeing double and swerving on the road, and then having the sensation of "waking up" at a light with a flat tire.

The MRI machine, is even better than the mammogram machine. I get wrapped in a nice warm blankie, close my eyes, and I'm quite comfortable, letting the machine examine my brain. The mood music (consisting of loud buzzes) was rather monotonous, but other than that, when it comes to sleeping with machines, the MRI is certainly a strong favorite. I like a machine that cares more about my brain than my boobs. Yes, a definite candidate for Mr. December.

I hadn't even realized until after we were done, that the doctor had been worried about the possibility of a brain tumor. The MRI did reveal a small growth on my Pituitary Gland. The doctor wasn't surprised because this was consistent with her recent blood work findings.

She assured me there were no brain tumors. The Pituitary Gland isn't technically your "brain" and this growth could most definitely be treated. "If you have any other unusual neurological problems, be sure and call me right away," she tells me.

Unusual neurological problems? Well, that's a big bucket load of possibility! People have told me my whole life that I have a very strange brain! It would be unusual for me to act normal! The fact that I'm now completely paranoid about a brain abnormality is exactly the way my normally abnormal brain works!

December 16 2pm

My face feels all tingly. Could that be a sign of brain disease? I had assumed it was because I went overboard with one of those facial hair removal electric razors last week and now the little hairs are growing back in. I don't know why I did it. I saw the razor in Walmart and had to buy it. I didn't even know there were such things as facial hair razors for women. I thought I'd just try a little section of my cheek. And then I couldn't stop. I did my whole face to keep everything even. And now it's all going to grow back and be stubbly and I'll look like a man!

Speaking of the person I blame this all on, Ryan called yesterday and wanted to know if I'd made a decision about going to Glenwood Springs. For once, I was completely honest and told him he'd ruined my life. I was going to have to shave my face for the rest of my life and I'd never be able to kiss anyone again without feeling paranoid. Ryan was very, very sorry. He even wanted to get back together to prove to me that he still liked to kiss me. Even though I know Ryan wasn't trying to be mean when he suggested I shave my upper lip and even though I need a Mr. December, I was very firm in my decision. No.

December 16 6pm

I have a splitting headache and my lower jaw feels numb. I don't think it's about the shaved face. This must be another brain malfunction. I call my doctor. It's outside of office hours.

"In case of emergency, hang up and dial 911."

Though I feel hesitant, I call 911 and explain the situation.

"We're going to send someone over to check it out."

Five minutes later the paramedics arrive in flashing ambulances. I hope the neighbors aren't watching.

There isn't one guy, there are six. And they are all really, really cute! This is like some personal bachelorette party complete with Chippendale men. Is this a dream? I half-way expect these guys to start dancing! They're all there in uniform being very attentive, taking my pulse and blood pressure. I'm sure my heart rate must be going up a bit! If I'd known I was going to get this kind of attention I would have called 911 a long time ago and made sure I was wearing something other than sweats! I'm not even wearing any makeup!

"I didn't expect so many of you!"

I wonder if it would be inappropriate to take a picture. Six sexy paramedics – I can pretend at least one of these guys is Mr. December.

As five of the cuties are gathered around asking me questions, a sixth goes upstairs. Apparently, it must be protocol for someone to go up and check your medicine cabinet to find out what kind of drugs the poor victim is on. Not that I don't want a cute guy in my bedroom, but I'm not prepared. My room is a mess! And right in the vanity area --where my prescriptions are stored -- is where I've left my underwear---dirty underwear! Inside out!

That's not all. My little stash of drugs includes Ambien, Lexapro, and – oh dear – a vaginal cream antibiotic. That's right. Despite the fact that I've been having no sex, I somehow managed to contract a vaginal infection. That's just what I want to discuss with some hot, young paramedic.

191

Scotty arrives home to all the commotion. The paramedics tell me it doesn't look like a stroke. (I'm very grateful that they do not question me further about the vaginal cream.) They offer to give me a ride to the hospital if I'd like to be checked out by a doctor. I look over at Scotty. I hate leaving him home alone, but he seems concerned about me. "I think you should go." he says adamantly. "I'll be fine."

December 16 10pm

In between a Parent/Teacher meeting and needing to pick his girls up from a football game, Michael has come to pick me up from the emergency room and give me a ride home.

"What happened?" He sounds very worried.

"Total false alarm. I just wanted some attention." I tell him that the doctors checked me out. The numbness in my face is minimal – probably a result of grinding my teeth. The growth on my pituitary gland is no biggie, literally. It's nowhere near the nerves that would affect my face.

"You're such a good friend." I tell Michael. "You're my hero."

"Are you drunk?" I understand why Michael would wonder this. My eyes are red with strain and I'm so exhausted I can barely keep my eyes open. My words seem a little slurred, too, from this numbness.

"No, I'm not drunk. Just really, really, tired." I close my eyes and think about how grateful I am for Michael and his car with the nice heated seats. Suddenly, I have an epiphany and smile a little.

"What are you thinking about?" Michael asks.

I'm remembering the whole plot of When Harry Met Sally. Sally had been distressed about her old boyfriend's marriage when she turned to her friend, Harry, for comfort. It was the turning point for her. When she realized it was her friend, Harry, who she really loved.

"I'm thinking about my book," I tell him. "I have an idea about how it might end."

December 16 10:30 pm

"Mom, what's wrong with you?" Scotty seems unusually worried when I get home.

"I'm fine, Scotty. Total false alarm."

192

"This morning I couldn't wake you up. And then, when you drove me to school, you were driving all over the road. I didn't think you'd make it home without getting in an accident."

"What are you talking about? I don't remember any of that!"

"Yeah. You'd fallen asleep on the couch and I kept telling you it was time to drive me to school, and then when you finally got up, you just said something about Pinocchio."

"Pinocchio?"

"Yeah, and then you got in the car, but you kept swerving and driving on the curb."

"Why didn't you tell me to stop?"

"I did! But you weren't paying any attention to me!"

Oh my God! This is terrible! I can't believe I put Scotty in danger like that! I'm a terrible mother! And now I'm more worried than ever about what kind of crazy person I am. Obviously, something must be very wrong with my brain.

December 19

I have a doctor's appointment with an endocrinologist at last! I'm hoping she can give me some answers. My family has been very worried about me. Dad is recovering, himself from surgery last month, and the last thing anyone needs is to worry about me. I'm sure the doctors will be able to figure out some kind of explanation for my crazy behavior. I haven't been driving, which is a real nuisance, and I'm having more trouble than ever concentrating at work. I blame it on brain problems, but I have to be careful. This might gain me sympathy points, but isn't exactly a good thing to have on the ol' resume.

The doctor looks over the paperwork that's been sent over.

"It appears your symptoms are consistent with someone who is peri-menopausal."

PERI-MENOPAUSAL? ARE YOU SERIOUS? Maybe it's the peri-menopausal symptoms that are making me want to scream right now and strangle this quack, but I don't think there are too many peri-menopausal women that take their sons on a little joy ride and can't even remember doing it.

"What about the elevated numbers from the pituitary growth?"

"Well we may have to do some additional tests," the doctor answers calmly.

"What about the double vision and the driving incident that I can't remember?"

"I don't know what may have caused that," she answers, "but the growth on your pituitary gland is too small to be hitting the optic nerve."

I know I should be relieved that I don't have any big tumor that needs surgery, but I want answers! And going back and telling my friends and family that all this worry and fuss is *menopause* is simply unacceptable.

December 27

"I'm sure it was the Ambien, probably because it was mixed with the Lexapro." I tell Michael.   After describing my "driving incident" to a friend, she'd asked me if I had been taking Ambien. I've been taking Ambien every night for almost 2 months. Sure enough, when I started doing a little internet research on this, I discovered that "sleep-driving" and other odd sleep-walking behaviors have been reported by people taking Ambien. There are actually quite a few instances of "sleep-eating," too – people that raid their refrigerators at night, eating all kinds of weird things. After endless tests to rule out anything else, the doctors agreed that Ambien was the most likely culprit.

"I'm glad I'm not dying, but I feel terrible that I was a negligent mother. I could have killed my son!"

"But you didn't. You're fine. He's fine. Everyone's fine."

Michael's right. I'm so lucky.

"So we're on for New Year's Eve, right?" I ask him.

"Sounds like a plan."

December 29

I hear noises out in the front and peek out my window. Brody is there with his snow-blower, clearing the snow off of my driveway! He knows I hate shoveling. I once had told him how chivalrous I thought it was when neighbors helped each other with shoveling. I'd heard that strong men like to help single women with that kind of thing and I was plotting with Brody, asking him if he thought I should act a little more damsel-in-distress-like so that my neighbors would take pity and shovel my driveway. I said I could start a new movement "Random acts of shovelry."

That had been over a year ago and I'd forgotten all about the conversation, but apparently Brody had remembered, because he has made the 15 minute drive through the snow with his snow-blower to clear my driveway.

I quickly get my winter coat on and run outside.

"Brody! My shovelrous knight!"

He turns off the machine so he can hear me and I give him a big hug.

"Well, someone's gotta teach you to give a proper blow job," he jokes. Then he turns back on the machine, wiggling his hips and performing crazy antics. He adjusts the blower so that the snow blows right in my face, and I scream and run out of the way, laughing.

Things hadn't been the same between us since last summer – I suppose neither one of us had entirely forgotten the hurt of that night at Wahoos. We'd talked a little, but the playful banter had been lost, and I'd missed my friend. I guess you could say his shovelrous act "broke the ice." Brody was back!

December 31 8am

It's a gorgeous final day of 2008. I'm at the Walnut Café in Boulder, breakfasting with Jeannine. We have a great discussion about relationships, as we usually do. Jeannine is back together with her boyfriend, Scott, and seems very happy. I'm happy for her. I share with her my plans for midnight – leaving my final adventure and Mr. December for this last night of the year. It's a bit risky, but, hey, that's what this year is all about, right? Jeannine approves of my plan.

Jeannine tells me she has something for me. She hands me an envelope and inside is a certificate she's made up: "Adventurer Extraordinaire – Yvette Francino". She's arranged photos of my different adventures on the certificate and gotten signatures from many of my *Rebuilder* friends, including, Boy Toy Chet, and Hubby Zach. The thoughtful gift moves me more than Jeannine can realize and I feel that warmth again. That feeling of being loved. What a beautiful friend she is.

December 31 7pm

I'm at my friend, Janelle's, New Year's Eve Party. There aren't very many people here. "Hubby" Zach's already here when I arrive. He

195

doesn't know any of these people, but when I'd invited him to join me, he'd agreed. As always, he looks totally dashing. That blue shirt brings out the blue of his eyes. I'm looking good tonight, too. I'm wearing some of my great new Christmas loot – the fitted black sweater from Megan and the bright red scarf that Matt brought me back from Nepal. And, as an accessory, the little gold bracelet with the engraved 'I love you' that I got from Scotty on Valentines Day.

December 31 10:45 pm

It feels a little rude to leave before midnight, especially because there aren't many people at this party, but Zach and I had told Janelle we'd had other plans at midnight. We walk out to our cars and Zach gives me a long hug with a little squeeze at the end. "Why don't you stay until midnight?" Zach asks. He's on his way to another party.

"I have plans, too!" I tell him. "I have my final adventure tonight with Mr. December at midnight!"

"Oh, really?" Zach says. "Are you going to tell me about this mystery man?"

"Not now. You have a party to get to. We'll compare notes in the New Year."

"Sounds good. Happy New Year, Honey." I smile at the use of "Honey" ever since the Wedding date.

"You too, Hun. Find someone at that party to kiss at midnight. I'll send you a virtual kiss text message."

"Will Mr. December approve of that?"

"Yeah, no problem. Mr. December isn't the jealous type."

December 31 Midnight

Oh what a comfortable bed I have. I stretch out like a satisfied cat. I've just sent Chet, Zach, Brody, Ian, and Michael virtual kisses using text messaging. Michael's expecting it and responds with a big, "Mwah!" He's with his daughter, Morgan, tonight, but last time we'd talked we'd agreed to a virtual midnight kiss. Brody replied, going beyond virtual kisses, doing some virtual fondling. Typical Brody. I'm so glad we're friends again.

I've been spending the last hour creating my 2008 slide show and setting it to the music of Auld Lang Syne, and I'm quite pleased

196

with the results. Digital photos, all nicely organized by month, serve nicely to remind me of this incredible year.

Looking up at me from the computer screen, I see Boy Toy Chet with me in Phoenix and Michael with me at the Shakespeare Festival. I see Zach with me on hikes and snowshoeing and of course, the wedding. There are photos of my beautiful kids, Megan, Chris, Matt, and Scotty. I find my parents and siblings and even an ultrasound photo of the newest member of the clan, due in July. There are photos of more than my designated adventures or men of the month. Events I'd forgotten about. There's a photo of that artistic design the barista drew in my mocha during my first chai chat with Jeannine. And the "I Love You" carved in the tree at the Frozen Dead Guy festival. There's that muddy trail that Ann and I trudged through in Costa Rica, those turquoise-shaded waves I jumped in with my new friends in Cancun, the red rocks of Garden of the Gods that Scotty, Matt, and I hiked through.

My "Adventure" this month? To be home in bed at midnight with someone I love. To be with someone who loves and accepts me for exactly who I am. Ever since my divorce, I've avoided being home in an empty house. And nothing could be worse than being home alone on New Year's Eve. Especially this year. I've been doing everything in my power to avoid being alone. The search for love has been on since January 1. Here I am on December 31rst, finding it, at last.

I see it in every photo. I feel it. It's that swelling in my chest that comes from pride in my children, from gratefulness for my friends and family, from awe at the beauty in the world. It's that emotion that brings those happy tears to my eyes – the same tears that came at the wedding, or when I learned I was going to be a Grandma, or this morning at breakfast with Jeannine. That feeling – I've experienced it countless times this year. How could I not recognize it? It's what I've been searching for. It's love.

I read my journals and look at these photos and realize I have more adventure and love in my life than I ever thought possible. Who's to judge whether or not an adventure is boring or exciting? Who decides whether or not it's better to listen to the devil or listen to the angel? Who says an adventure has to be scary? Maybe it's as simple as facing a fear – whether that be a fear of death or a fear of loneliness. The adventure isn't about the risk or the fear. It's about the joy that comes from facing our challenges and living our passions.

Every day is an adventure. Every relationship is an opportunity to love. I've been so busy looking around for some soul mate, I almost missed the love that was right in front of my nose. The love that's available to me every day!

Angel: You're talking about God's love, aren't you Dear?
Devil: What a crock of shit! You don't have a Mr. December! This is just a wimpy ending to a wimpy book! You have no one in your bed!

You're both wrong! It's me! I'm the one with her photos and journals, all stored nicely on my very hard drive. I'm Mr. December. I'm the one she loves. I'm the one she lives with happily ever after. Tell them, Yvette.

I think back to that day when I explained Laptop Guy to my brother, Neal. *"Laptop Guy is **me**."*

And with the utmost security of knowing that I have truly found love, I answer, *"Yes Laptop Guy. It's been you all along."*

Resolution Review

1. *Have An Adventure Each Month – Check!*
2. *Fall in Love – Check!*
3. *Write a Book – Check!*

And, of course, live happily ever after.........

Epilogue

Last night I spent New Year's Eve enjoying the evening with three cute guys. Two of them were the children of the man I'm dating, but they were very cute, just the same. As for the man – Jason – well, he's much more than cute.

The *The Laptop Dancer Diaries* took place in 2008. In 2009, I did some dating, but with little expectation of finding a mate. I was content with my life and felt ready to accept a fate of singleness. Then for some reason, last month, I got the urge to explore the world of online dating one more time before I crossed over into that decade I'd been dreading for so long – the fifties.

The first profile I came across was Jason's. His profile included only a couple of sentences but contained just the adjectives and descriptions that were most important to me... playful, confident, love of children, spiritual. He was 48, so entirely age-appropriate. His face smiled out from his profile photo and my heart felt that little tingle of hope. Of course, if you've read the book, you know my history with online dating is pretty dismal. I have learned people are usually much better in their profiles than in real life.

Not so with Jason. Our first meeting was at a cozy pub that he'd suggested. We sat in front of the fire and chatted and I immediately liked him. I always thought when I found the right guy, I'd know it. There would be no questions or fears or worries. I'd just know he was right. And that's exactly what I felt.

Amazingly, Jason liked me, too. Two days later, I was having a romantic dinner at his house. Soon after that, I was relaxing in his hot tub, feeling snowflakes on my face, looking up at the sky and feeling like I'd found a piece of heaven.

The happy surprises continued as I got to know Jason better. His children are polite and sweet – such little gentlemen who charm me with their smiles and giggles. Last night, Jason let me share in the good-night rituals, and when 11-year-old Connor reached out his arms for a hug and kiss good-night, I choked back a tear – I was so moved by his innocent acceptance and affection. Could I already love this little family when I've only just met them?

My relationship with Jason is too new for me to declare that I've fallen in love. Those words scare me. What if he doesn't feel the same way about me? I don't think I can survive another broken heart.

But I think about that innocent affection that Connor showed me and know I want to be like that. I want to love without fear. If it doesn't last forever, it will hurt, but I'll survive. And if I don't take the risk, I will never know what might have been. Even if it only lasts a month or a week or a day or an hour ... I want to know the joy of loving someone.

I started this book looking for a cookbook approach to falling in love and I think I've found the answers. Find out who you are. Take risks. Live life to the fullest. Live like you are the protagonist of a book. Love all the people around you – your friends, your family, your pets and even your laptop, if you want. Love God, life, the ocean and the mountains. Figure out what's right for you and don't let anyone – not even your inner-angel or inner-devil guilt you into doing anything you don't want to do. Love yourself.

And when that right person comes along, love like a child that's never been hurt -- reach out your arms and give of your heart. Trust that whether it lasts for a minute or for a lifetime, it will be worth it.

And *that's* the secret for falling in love.

About the Author

Yvette Francino lives in Superior, Colorado with her 15-year-old son, Scotty, their disobedient dog, Chloe, and her laptop, Laptop Guy.

Yvette's next project is the "Mostly Untrue" version of *The Laptop Dancer Diaries* and welcomes your help and participation.

For more information about Yvette or *The Laptop Dancer Diaries* please visit:

http://www.yvettefrancino.com
http://www.thelaptopdancerdiaries.com

Made in the USA
San Bernardino, CA
20 October 2014